THINKERS
50

Management

Management

Cutting-Edge Thinking to Engage and Motivate
Your Employees for Success

Withdrawn/ABCL

STUART CRAINER + DES DEARLOVE

New York   Chicago   San Francisco   Athens   London   Madrid
Mexico City   Milan   New Delhi   Singapore   Sydney   Toronto

1 2 3 4 5 6 7 8 9 0   DOC/DOC   1 9 8 7 6 5 4 3

ISBN   978-0-07-182783-6
MHID   0-07-182783-8

e-ISBN 978-0-07-182784-3
e-MHID   0-07-182784-6

Library of Congress Cataloging-in-Publication Data

Crainer, Stuart.
  Thinkers50 management : cutting-edge thinking to engage and motivate your employees for success / by Stuart Crainer and Des Dearlove.
     pages cm
  Includes index.
  ISBN 978-0-07-182783-6 (alk. paper) — ISBN 0-07-182783-8 (alk. paper)
  1. Employee motivation. 2. Personnel management. 3. Management.
  I. Dearlove, Des. II. Title.
  HF5549.5.M63C73 2014
  658.3'14—dc23
                                                         2013030618

McGraw-Hill Education books are available at special quantity discounts to use as premiums and sales promotions or for use in corporate training programs. To contact a representative, please visit the Contact Us pages at www.mhprofessional.com.

Contents

CONTENTS

Introduction

In the late 1980s we met an octogenarian who had just visited one of London's more obscure art galleries. Despite living in the city, we had never heard of it. He talked enthusiastically and knowledgably about the wonders he had seen. In conversation, he talked about meeting Freud in Vienna when he was a child, his passion for the novels of Trollope, and how he reread Jane Austen every year to remind himself of what great writing was. He also told us of arriving in London from Vienna and working at *The Economist*. Later, in 1937, he settled in the United States and forged a unique reputation as the creator of modern management. His name was Peter Ferdinand Drucker (1909–2005).

Years later, in 2001, when we first came up with the idea of ranking the world's management thinkers, his was the name that topped our list. In 2003, when we compiled our second ranking, once again he commanded the number one slot. Peter Drucker died on November 11, 2005, but his legacy lives on.

Drucker was the man who almost single-handedly turned management into a discipline worthy of study, who powerfully revealed the centrality of management to any organization, who created the managerial job description—and a good deal more.

In his 1954 book *The Practice of Management*, Drucker establishes five basics of the managerial role: to set objectives, to organize, to motivate and communicate, to measure, and to develop people. "The function which distinguishes the manager above all others is his educational one," he wrote. "The one contribution he is uniquely expected to make is to give others vision and ability to perform. It is vision and moral responsibility that, in the last analysis, define the manager." This morality is reflected in the five areas identified by Drucker "in which practices are required to ensure the right spirit throughout management organization":

1. There must be high performance requirements, there must be no condoning of poor or mediocre performance, and rewards must be based on performance.
2. Each management job must be a rewarding job in itself rather than just a step on the promotion ladder.
3. There must be a rational and just promotion system.
4. Management needs a "charter" spelling out clearly who has the power to make "life-and-death" decisions affecting a manager, and there should be some way for a manager to appeal to a higher court.
5. In its appointments, management must demonstrate that it realizes that integrity is the one absolute require-

ment of a manager, the one quality that he has to bring with him and cannot be expected to acquire later on.

Drucker's aspirations for managers and the profession of management remain important more than half a century later. So, too, does the importance invested in management by Drucker. It took management to build the railways, to tend the Hanging Gardens of Babylon, to build any of the great monuments of history. Equally, it takes management to run the great organizations and endeavors of our time, from multinational corporations to the Indian railway system, to the United Kingdom's National Health Service, to the U.S. Army.

Management matters. It shapes the world. It is the vital barrier that protects us from chaos. It is a calling and an enabling force.

Peter Drucker was right about the importance of management—and much else.

This book brings together the big ideas on management, past and present, and makes sense of them through contemporary eyes. Along the way, we feature the views and insights of the people we have interviewed over recent years as part of the Thinkers50's endeavors to scan, rank, and share the best management ideas. They include Tammy Erickson, Daniel Goleman, Lynda Gratton, Gary Hamel, Sylvia Ann Hewlett, Rosabeth Moss Kanter, John Kotter, Henry Mintzberg, Dan Pink, Doug Ready, and many more.

Stuart Crainer and Des Dearlove
Thinkers50 Founders

How We Got Here

Management is all-embracing. "There are, of course, differences in management between different organizations—mission defines strategy, after all, and strategy defines structure. But the differences between managing a chain of retail stores and managing a Roman Catholic diocese are amazingly fewer than either retail executives or bishops realize," Peter Drucker observed. "The differences are mainly in application rather than in principles. The executives of all these organizations spend, for instance, about the same amount of their time on people problems—and the people problems are almost always the same.

"So whether you are managing a software company, a hospital, a bank, or a Boy Scout organization, the differences apply to only about 10 percent of your work. This 10 percent is determined by the organization's specific mission, its specific culture, its specific history and its specific vocabulary. The rest is pretty much interchangeable."[1]

Even though management is global and timeless, a neat definition is elusive. "Management is . . ." leads to quizzical silence and furrowed brows whether you are on a factory floor in Nebraska, in a Harvard seminar room, or in a trading hall in Hong Kong.

According to Wikipedia, "Management is the act of getting people together to accomplish desired goals and objectives." True, but there is much more to management than that. The attraction—and the trouble—is that management is multifaceted. Pinning it down is like nailing Jell-O. It is marketing. It is strategy. It is inspiring people. It is budgeting. It is organizing projects and commitments. It is a complex, highly personal, and now truly global calling.

With all this complexity, it is no surprise that the historical and theoretical strands that make up contemporary management are many and varied. The great management thinkers are drawn from a bewildering variety of disciplines and professions. There are economists, such as Harvard Business School's Michael Porter; psychologists, such as Edgar Schein of the Massachusetts Institute of Technology; sociologists, such as Rosabeth Moss Kanter of Harvard Business School; management consultants, such as Bruce Henderson and Marvin Bower; engineers aplenty, from Frederick Taylor to the civil engineering–trained Tom Peters; and even a nuclear physicist, the clarinet-playing would-be politician Kenichi Ohmae.

Indeed, what increasingly sets management apart as a profession is that it is amenable to being driven by ideas. In management, theories make a difference; ideas are put to work and can change the lives of millions of people. The obverse of this is that if ideas don't work, they are quickly consigned to history. This explains the continual churn of ideas. They come and go with increasing rapidity.

Mining Management

The first to effectively codify management was Henri Fayol (1841–1925), who spent his entire working career with the French mining company Commentry-Fourchambault-Décazeville. He saved that company from the brink of bankruptcy and was managing director between 1888 and 1918.

Along the way, Fayol developed 14 "general principles of management." The following, he said, were the universal characteristics of management:

1. Division of work
2. Authority and responsibility
3. Discipline
4. Unity of command
5. Unity of direction
6. Subordination of individual interest to general interest
7. Remuneration of employees
8. Centralization
9. The scalar chain
10. Order
11. Equity
12. Stability of personnel
13. Initiative
14. Esprit de corps

Fayol's 14 principles were what concerned managers or what should have concerned managers. To ensure that they were put into effective practice, Fayol said that managers needed to plan, organize, command, coordinate, and control. As a summary of what the job of management is, this remains largely true in the twenty-first century.

Of course, over time the emphasis on each of these aspects is turned up or down depending on circumstances. Looking back, it is possible to detect a pattern. Periods of fascination with the human side of enterprise (the soft areas of motivation, development, and culture) are interspersed with periods when the hard side—analysis, data, strategy, structure, and processes—prevails.

Management as Science

In the early twentieth century, the hard side dominated. Although Fayol's ideas largely failed to find a mass audience, scientific management became the first international management theory. Created by Frederick Taylor (1856–1915), it was built around the measurement of activities. Managers held stopwatches and knew how long jobs should take.

In terms of management, Taylor brought analytical vigor to the workplace. Before Taylor, no one had scientifically analyzed the nature of work. Taylor looked at work anew. Scientific management was the Total Quality Management (TQM) of its day. Taylor's work was known and devoured in Japan. In Russia, Lenin was a fan. In France, his champion was the metallurgist Henri Le Chatelier. By the time of Taylor's death, two editions of the French translation of *The Principles of Scientific Management* had been printed and 4,000 had been sold (another 3,000 had been, according to Chatelier, "gratuitously distributed").

The development of Taylor's theories went in tandem with Henry Ford's development of the production line: Ford's assembly line was scientific management at work. Peter Drucker has cited Taylor's thinking as "the most lasting contribution America has made to Western thought since the *Federalist Papers.*" Wasn't Henry Ford a bigger deal? No, says Drucker. The assembly line was simply a logical extension of scientific management.[2]

People First

As mass production created the first generation of modern managers, attention switched to the human side of enterprise. Most notably, experiments at Western Electric's Hawthorne plant in Cicero, Illinois, between 1927 and 1932 sought to understand the behavior of people in the new industrial environment.

The Hawthorne Studies began with experiments in which the lighting in the factory was altered. The theory was that brighter light would raise morale and, as a result, increase productivity. Elton Mayo (1880–1949) and his researchers set out to establish the lighting level that maximized productivity without being prohibitively expensive. This seemed straightforward, simply a question of finding the balance between cost and effect.

Hawthorne workers were separated into two groups. In one group the lighting levels were increased, and productivity increased. In the other group the lighting remained at its normal level, and productivity increased. Lighting levels were further increased, but still the productivity levels in the two groups remained much the same.

This seemed surprisingly inconclusive. How could productivity rise when the lighting remained exactly the same?
The researchers therefore started reducing lighting levels. They
reduced the lighting in one group drastically, and productivity
increased. Eventually, the light was reduced to extreme dusk-
iness. It was expected that the workers would be depressed
and irritable working in moonlight. In fact, their productivity
remained at a similar level and sometimes increased. To prove
the point, two workers were isolated in a very small room with
minimal lighting. Their productivity continued at a healthy level.

The researchers shook their heads and contemplated
what all this meant. They were confused but, being researchers,
returned with a more complicated experiment. In the factory's
relay assembly test room, a group of six women who assembled
telephone relay switches were selected and isolated in a test
room. There they were diligently observed. Conditions were
changed and tinkered with. However, nothing seemed to reduce
productivity.

The conclusion from the research team was that they had
missed something, which turned out to be the relationships,
attitudes, feelings, and perceptions of the people involved. The
research program had revolved around selecting small groups of
workers to be studied. This, not surprisingly, made the workers
feel special. For the first time they actually felt that management
was interested in them. The second effect was that the people felt
that they belonged to a select team. They identified with their
group. "The desire to stand well with one's fellows, the so-called
human instinct of association, easily outweighs the merely individual interest and the logic of reasoning upon which so many spu-
rious principles of management are based," commented Mayo.

Beyond Departments

A Japanese manager quoted in Richard Pascale's *Managing on the Edge* made an important observation: "There is nothing wrong with the findings. But the Hawthorne experiments look at human behavior from the wrong perspective. Your thinking needs to build from the idea of empowering workers, placing responsibility closest to where the knowledge resides, using consistently honored values to draw the separate individuals together. The Hawthorne experiments imply smug superiority, parent-to-child assumptions. This is not a true understanding."[3]

Rebutting such assumptions was a gaunt Boston spinster, Mary Parker Follett (1868–1933), who was discussing issues such as teamwork and responsibility (now reborn as empowerment) in the first decades of the twentieth century. Follett was a female liberal humanist in an era dominated by reactionary males intent on mechanizing the world of business.

The thrust of Follett's thinking was that people are central to any business activity or, indeed, to any other activity. "I think we should undepartmentalize our thinking in regard to every problem that comes to us," said Follett. "I do not think that we have psychological and ethical and economic problems. We have human problems, with psychological, ethical and economical aspects, and as many others as you like."[4]

During World War II, the human side again took a backseat. Nations focused on production no matter what. But in the 1950s the softer side of theory was again to the fore with the human relations school of thinkers, including Douglas McGregor, Abraham Maslow, and Frederick Herzberg. In the early 1960s, the hard side of strategy and structure took over. Alfred P. Sloan's 1963 book *My Years with General Motors* provided an organizational coda. Strategic management with its focus on analysis and tools such as the Boston matrix ruled the managerial roost.

The hard side dominated throughout the 1960s and 1970s with only occasional intermissions, such as Henry Mintzberg's *The Nature of Managerial Work* in 1973. In the 1980s the soft side revived. The Japanese were the role models, and they, as Richard Pascale and Anthony Athos pointed out in *The Art of Japanese Management*, were not the ruthless strategists we had been led to believe but were driven by imponderables such as corporate values. Leadership returned to the agenda; marketing and customer service were rediscovered. Quality, which began life as arid statistical control, was reinterpreted as a human discipline.

The early 1990s saw a resurgence of the hard scientific school through reengineering. With reengineering soon used largely as a euphemism for downsizing, the emphasis returned to the soft side of intuition and values, people as resources rather than staff. In 1997 McKinsey set the agenda by describing what it called the war for talent.

During the last 20 years, the soft and hard pattern has become blurred. Hard subjects such as the rise of big data rest alongside the rise of global teams and the challenges of motivating a more skeptical younger generation. The modern manager has to be a master of both sides: the art and science of management.

Sense Making

To make sense of this ebb and flow we have identified nine concepts that are the central focus of today's management thinking:

1. **What managers do (Chapter 2).** Ambiguity and isolation are the twin fears voiced by CEOs in their more candid moments. Ambiguity stems from the fact that the more senior you are in the executive scale, the less your job is mapped out for you. Indeed, this troubling lack of clear identity lies at the heart of management. Any understanding of management must begin with an appreciation of how managers spend and should spend their time.

2. **Engaging people (Chapter 3).** Research suggests there is a chronic lack of engagement among contemporary employees throughout the world. Understanding this requires that we better understand the evolution of management thinking around motivation and put it in a modern context. Sylvia Ann Hewlett and Gary Hamel are among those leading the intellectual charge.

3. **Managing processes (Chapter 4).** From Frederick Taylor's scientific management and Henry Ford to modern-day production, the processes that lie behind organizational life have exercised the best minds. We trace the lineage of ideas from Henry Ford via W. Edwards Deming and reengineering to the present day.

4. **Measuring performance (Chapter 5).** A one-stop measure for managerial performance is elusive, perhaps impossible. In the meantime, organizations worldwide have embraced the balanced scorecard as a managerial measure.

5. **Managing change (Chapter 6).** Our age does not have a monopoly on change; societies and the business world

have always changed and improved. What is new, however, is our awareness that the process of change can, for better or worse, be managed.

6. **Managing talent (Chapter 7).** The war for talent was announced in the 1990s. Talent has won. But what does this mean for those who attempt to manage and lead talented people? Doug Ready is among those proposing solutions.

7. **Managing globally (Chapter 8).** Globalization is a fact of corporate life rather than a decorative addition. How does this change the nature of management? How do cultural perceptions and reality affect what managers now do and think?

8. **Managing emotionally (Chapter 9).** It has long been recognized that management is a very human science. From Howard Gardner's multiple intelligences to Daniel Goleman's concept of emotional intelligence and Dan Pink on the art of selling, we examine the emotions behind performance.

9. **Managing millennials (Chapter 10).** One of the biggest issues facing managers is how to manage the expectations, perceptions, and behavior of the new generation entering the workforce. Tammy Erickson and Lynda Gratton are among those who have made suggestions.

CHAPTER 2

What
Managers Do

Amid the intellectual jousting of academic research, it is interesting and perhaps worrying that what managers actually do is often overlooked. It is notable, if somewhat bizarre, that the actual tasks undertaken by people in the course of their work have been examined so little. This is particularly true for managerial work. Examinations of what managers really do are few and far between even now. The most significant is Henry Mintzberg's study in the early 1970s that led to his groundbreaking book *The Nature of Managerial Work*. Mintzberg, of Canada's McGill University, has consistently lamented the lack of substantial scholarship about "managers and the essential work they do in organizations."

The conclusions of Mintzberg's research would have shocked and appalled Frederick Taylor: Mintzberg found that managers flitted from task to task, job to job, in an apparently inefficient manner. Instead of spending time contemplating the long term, managers, Mintzberg found, were slaves to the moment, moving from task to task with every move dogged by another diversion, another call. The median time spent on any single issue was a mere nine minutes. In *The Nature of Managerial Work*, Mintzberg identifies the characteristics of the manager at work:

- Performs a great quantity of work at an unrelenting pace
- Undertakes activities marked by variety, brevity, and fragmentation
- Has a preference for issues that are current, specific, and nonroutine
- Prefers verbal rather than written means of communication
- Acts within a web of internal and external contacts
- Is subject to heavy constraints but can exert some control over the work

From these observations, Mintzberg identified the manager's "work roles" as follows:

Interpersonal roles

> **Figurehead:** representing the organization or unit to outsiders
>
> **Leader:** motivating subordinates and unifying effort
>
> **Liaiser:** maintaining lateral contacts

Informational roles

Monitor: of information flows

Disseminator: of information to subordinates

Spokesman: transmission of information to outsiders

Decisional roles

Entrepreneur: initiator and designer of change

Disturbance handler: handling nonroutine events

Resource allocator: deciding who gets what and who will
do what

Negotiator: negotiating

This may sound familiar. Mintzberg revisited the book in the first decade of the twenty-first century in *Managing*. We asked him why so few books have been written about what managers actually do.

How can that be with all the management scholars in universities around the world?

Mind-blowing, isn't it? I could only find one person, a guy in Sweden, who was devoting much of his career to researching the practice of management. Then there is Rosemary Stuart in the United Kingdom. Why aren't others doing it? It's an interesting question. Perhaps managers are regarded as gods and you don't dare approach them. We asked Stuart about this.

But you've pointed out often that they are not gods.

Yes, they are ordinary, flawed human beings like the rest of us. I think that researchers in business schools these days are being drawn to narrower and harder subjects they can be more "rigorous" about. There's nothing rigorous about most of this research. A lot of it is nonsense, but in the sense of academic journals, it is rigorous with fancy hypotheses, tested in all kinds of ways that never, or rarely, bring any insight. They don't look at things holistically, and they don't look at the big question. Or they shoot their mouths off about leadership without really getting into any depth.

Is that because leadership is seen as sexy while management is taken to be desperately mundane?
Yes. Doctors and surgeons refer to scut work. They turn to the nurse and say, "You close them up"; that's scut work. The narcissistic view of leadership has taken organizations off the rails.

Do you want to make management sexy, or do you just want to redress the balance between management and leadership?
Neither. I certainly don't want to make management sexy. I want it to be recognized as a basic, fundamental human activity, and I don't want the focus to be on management *versus* leadership. I think that's more of a corrective thing, to realize that leadership isn't better than management. I want people to recognize that one component of management is leadership but that there are lots of other components: information, action, how you involve yourself, how you connect, and all sorts of things.

Is it fair to say that leadership is too often portrayed as black or white, that there's good and there's bad but the reality of management is complicated and contextual: it's shades of gray?

One of my favorite conundrums is how you stay connected when the very fact of being a manager disconnects you from what you're managing. In other words, yesterday you were an engineer and today you're managing engineers, so you're no longer doing engineering. So how do you face that?

Given the time that has passed since your first book on managerial work, what has changed?

The content of managing changes all the time—what you're dealing with, how your industry is structured—but the process hasn't changed. The one big thing that I do talk about is the Internet and especially e-mail, but I think those forms of communications just reinforce problematic behavior. So I think they're just making it worse, but I don't think they're changing management fundamentally. One thing that I admit has changed is that management has been ignored in favor of leadership.

Haven't the changes in communication really affected the job of management? After all, the Internet and e-mail have made management more of a 24/7 job.

I'm not sure that it has changed. I agree that communication is a huge part of the job: managers spend 50 percent of their time, in some cases, on communication.

But if you go back to a study in the 1940s of Swedish managing directors, they were inundated with reports, they couldn't keep up, and there were no computers around. Communication has always been a big part of the job and remains a big part of the job, but I am not sure that's new. If you checked with managers 40 or 50 years ago, you would have found the same thing.

The ability to communicate through e-mail has certainly changed some practices, but managers who rely on e-mail to communicate with their people are in deep trouble. It is a narrow form of communication that's wonderful for getting a lot of data moved around quickly and for short things (that's why Twitter is its most appropriate form), but it's not the way to communicate fully, richly.

There's a generational thing in all this as well, though, isn't there? For the younger generation of managers, shallow and immediate seems to be fine. Anything wrong with that attitude?

It's whether that's going to prove to be good management, and that might be another factor behind the current crisis: people have been managing too superficially. The occupational hazard of managing is superficiality, and these things could make it worse.

The Pro Manager

Given the flitting nature of management identified by Mintzberg, there is perhaps an irony in the fact that recent years have seen the pressing of the case for management to be regarded and rec-ognized as a profession. At the forefront of this debate is the dean of Harvard Business School, Nitin Nohria, and the Harvard professor Rakesh Khurana.

Is management a profession? And if not, should it be? Should the MBA be regarded as a requirement to practice man-agement in the same way as the requirements for being a doc-tor or a lawyer? In his 2007 book *From Higher Aims to Hired Hands*, Khurana argued that business schools set out with the grand idea of professionalizing management, but that project remains unfinished.

"My argument is that, in addition to questions about the efficacy of the degree, most MBAs want their work to have meaning; they want to be professionals. But business schools are not providing some way for them to link their personal values to the work they are going to be doing," Khurana says.

Khurana is not the first B-school luminary to criticize his employers. Professors Henry Mintzberg at McGill and Jeffrey Pfeffer at Stanford have both been persistent thorns in the side of B-schools.

Khurana's criticism is measured and is the more damning for it. His book is an impressive tour of the social and intellectual history of American university business schools. It reveals how the desire to raise management first to a profession and later to a science has driven business education and shaped American management for more than a century.

The origins of the U.S. B-schools lie in the late nineteenth century, he argues, when members of an emerging managerial elite, seeking social status to match the wealth and power they had accrued, began working with major universities. The new

commercial barons set out to establish graduate business education programs paralleling those for medicine and law.

But to make management a profession, they faced serious
hurdles. They needed to codify knowledge that was relevant for
management practitioners and develop enforceable standards of
conduct. That was not easy.

Drawing on a rich set of archival material from business
schools, foundations, and academic associations, Khurana
traces how the fledgling U.S. B-schools confronted these challenges with varying strategies during the Progressive era and the
Depression, the postwar boom years, and the recent decades of
freewheeling capitalism. But Khurana's work is more than just a
historical odyssey; it is also a heartfelt plea for business schools
to rediscover their higher purpose.

The university-based business schools, including Harvard,
where Khurana is employed, were founded to train a professional class of managers akin to doctors and lawyers. But, he
argues forcefully, they have retreated from that goal. That has left
a moral vacuum at the center of business education and, arguably, management itself. That moral vacuum was all too evident
during the financial crisis of recent years. Indeed, many would
say it was the cause of the banking crisis.

Could the establishment of management as a profession
have prevented Enron, Lehman Brothers, and the other recent
(and periodic) corporate scandals? The answer is probably no,
any more than a professional code completely eliminates medical or legal malpractice. But a widely accepted code of conduct
taught by B-schools would at least raise the ethical bar. Certainly
it did not help that several of those involved in the scandals of

recent years, including Jeffrey Skilling, the former Enron CEO, were MBA holders.

Khurana argues that business schools have largely capitulated in the battle for professionalism and have become mere purveyors of a product, the MBA. The professional and moral ideals that once inspired their teaching have been eclipsed by a view that the only significant measure of managers is their ability to create shareholder value.

Ultimately, though, this is an abdication of responsibility. Khurana believes the time has come to upgrade the training of our future business leaders and complete the professionalization project.

"By denying students the opportunity of seeing their career as a profession, seeing meaning in their work, seeing their work as a calling, we are actually denying them the possibility of seeing how they can connect what they do to some larger purpose," he says.

Arguing the case for management's acceptance as a profession, Khurana and Nitin Nohria have proposed the equivalent of the Hippocratic Oath for managers. "If management were to be seen as a true profession guided by a broadly agreed upon and shared global code of business conduct, our expectations of the moral conduct of managers and their expectations in themselves would rise. This can be an important step in restoring the frayed trust in business and capitalism," say Khurana and Nohria.[1]

This spurred a group of second-year students in Harvard Business School's MBA program to create an MBA Oath as a way of establishing clear and unequivocal professional standards.

The oath combines the tone of the American Constitution with that of an annual report: "As a manager, my purpose is to serve the greater good by bringing people and resources together to create value that no single individual can create alone. Therefore I will seek a course that enhances the value my enterprise can create for society over the long term. I recognize my decisions can have far-reaching consequences that affect the well-being of individuals inside and outside my enterprise, today and in the future. As I reconcile the interests of different constituencies, I will face choices that are not easy for me and others."

Eight promises follow. They include "I will act with utmost integrity and pursue my work in an ethical manner" and "I will strive to create sustainable economic, social and environmental prosperity worldwide."

Some are skeptical. They include Henry Mintzberg: "If Jeff Skilling, the ex-president of Enron who is now in jail, was faced with this when he was at Harvard Business School, he would have signed in a flash. All this nonsense does is indicate how disconnected are the business schools from reality. Ethics is not some case study debated furiously by people utterly removed from the issues. Unfortunately, it becomes that when people so trained are given responsibility for corporations. As I note in *Managing*, management is a practice rooted in context, not a profession based on pronouncements."

Despite the profusion of pronouncements and their increasing volume, for managers context is king.

CHAPTER 3

Engaging
People

In the 1950s, the archetypal employee was "the man in the gray flannel suit," immortalized in Sloan Wilson's book of that name. Implicit to the career of the corporate man was the understanding that loyalty and solid performance brought job security. This was mutually beneficial. The executive gained a respectable income and a high degree of security; the company gained loyal, hardworking executives. Win, win.

This unspoken pact became known as the *psychological contract*. The originator of the phrase was the MIT-based social psychologist Edgar Schein. Schein's interest in the employee-employer relationship developed during the late 1950s. Schein noted the similarities between the brainwashing of prisoners of war he had witnessed during the Korean War and the corporate indoctrination carried out by the likes of GE and IBM.

"There were enormous similarities between the brainwashing of the POWs and the executives I encountered at MIT," Schein told us when we spoke. "I didn't see brainwashing as bad. What was bad were the values of the communists. If we don't like the values, we don't approve of brainwashing." The dynamics of groups and Schein's knowledge of brainwashing later led him to develop an interest in corporate culture, a term he is widely credited with inventing.

The psychological contract was built around loyalty. Executives were expected to be blindly loyal. "The most important single contribution required of an executive, certainly the most universal qualification, is loyalty [allowing] domination by the organization personality," noted Chester Barnard in *The Functions of the Executive* (1938). The word *domination* suggests the way Barnard saw the balance of power falling. Although loyalty is a positive quality, it can easily become blind. What if the corporate strategy is wrong or the company is engaged in unlawful or immoral acts? Also, there is the question of loyal to what. In the 1950s, corporate values were assumed rather than explored or questioned.

With careers neatly organized, executives were hardly encouraged to look over the corporate parapets to seek out broader viewpoints. The corporation became a self-contained and self-perpetuating world supported by a complex array of checks, systems, and hierarchies. The company was right. Customers, who existed in the ethereal world outside the organization, were often regarded as peripheral. In the 1950s, 1960s, and 1970s, no executive ever lost his or her job by delivering poor quality or indifferent service. Indeed, in some organizations, executives lost their jobs only by defrauding their employer or insulting their boss. Jobs for life was the refrain and, to a large extent for executives, the reality.

Clearly, such an environment was hardly conducive to the fostering of dynamic risk takers. The psychological contract rewarded the steady foot soldier, the safe pair of hands. It was hardly surprising, therefore, that when she came to examine corporate life for the first time in her 1977 book *Men and Women of the Corporation*, Rosabeth Moss Kanter found that the central characteristic expected of a manager was "dependability."

The reality was that the psychological contract placed a premium on loyalty rather than ability and allowed a great many poor performers to find corporate havens. It was also significant that the psychological contract was regarded as the preserve of management. Lower down the hierarchy, people were hired and fired with abandon no matter how great their loyalty.

That Was Then

Times change. The engagement of employees no longer is assumed. Survey after survey suggests that only a minority of employees are fully engaged with their work. A group of thinkers have sought to clarify what this means for managers and their organizations. Among those leading the way is Sylvia Ann Hewlett, founding president of the Center for Work-Life Policy, a nonprofit think tank in which she chairs the "Hidden Brain Drain," a task force of 50 global companies and organizations committed to fully realizing female and multicultural talent. In addition, she directs the Gender and Policy Program of the School of International and Public Affairs at Columbia University.

In good times, companies say that people are the most important asset. In bad times, they get rid of them. Is that a paradox or hypocrisy?

At the heart of the problem is that a lot of the top performers out there feel totally ignored and out of the loop. Their bosses are perhaps focusing on the clamoring clients or on the vaporizing bottom line. And these top performers feel that they're being taken for granted.

Many bosses seem to think that with a 10-plus percent rate of unemployment they can rely on their best people putting their nose to the grindstone and delivering 110 percent day in, day out. But that's not true: there's a lot of alienation, a lot of disengagement.

My sense is that 50 percent of the workforce is spending more than half of their time looking for the next job. I think the flight risk, as well as the productivity losses, that happen because bosses are out of touch with how their workers think and feel (even their best workers!) is enormous.

You have said that the loyalty rate among star performers has plunged from over 90 percent to about 53 percent. Why has that happened?

Top performers feel neglected, and many of them are struggling by working in companies with broken business models. There is massive turbulence in entire industries, and those working in such companies feel that they're not involved in figuring out how to help move the company forward. They also feel that somehow they're not nearly as important as they used to be. They're struggling by working within depleted teams, given that many of their peers might have been fired over the last couple of years.

If you are working in a company today, the odds are you're doing much more work with less help or resources. In our surveys, we find that 20 percent of employees are working nine hours more than just a year ago. So the pressures are intense and the recognition of effort is very low. Obviously there's a lot of disengagement, a lot of turning off of trust and loyalty to the company and its bosses.

How many people are totally engaged in their work?
Only about 10 to 20 percent of people in any organization are fully engaged. There's a mass of people who aren't really one way or another, and then there are people who are actively disengaged. A British study confirms that the engagement level of top performers is down 25 percent. This is dangerous.

Keep in mind that the top performers are the most mobile, the ones who can get new jobs easily. When a company lays off workers thinking it will be a boon to the bottom line, it is being myopic. The top talent, the people who were not laid off, are most likely to be among the survivors, the ones who will have to work harder as a result, and will feel underappreciated as a result. And these are the folks who can get jobs most easily on the outside, who can even cross over to other sectors.

The smart employer needs to place this task at the top of his or her agenda these days: be proactive about nurturing, supporting, and making sure your top talent knows they're important.

Are your observations and advice applicable to all industries?

I think right across the board. As we pick up our heads from the economic rubble and try to find renewal and growth going forward, no matter what sector you're in, it's your collective workforce brainpower that's going to be the big driver of success tomorrow.

And that's true in a basic industry, it's true certainly in science and technology, it's true in the media, and it's true on Wall Street or in the oldest firms in the City of London. It's really across the board; we now have a knowledge economy that's highly dependent on innovative thinking by top people to spur the next wave of corporate growth. Ignoring your best people right now is a definite business risk.

Do you see some companies that revere their top talent?

In the most recent research my team and I conducted, we focused on 30 different companies. Half of them are on Main Street, more locally owned; the other half are on Wall Street or in a larger city.

What we found is that there are some very important top-management interventions that really are working in terms of ratcheting up engagement, reigniting effort, making sure that people can really fire on all cylinders even in the middle of a great recession when perhaps bonuses are rare and pay raises are again something that many companies can't pony up.

Hamel and Engagement

Also prominent in the debate about employee engagement is Gary Hamel, coauthor with C. K. Prahalad of *Competing for the Future*. When we spoke with Hamel, what shined through was his passion for change. He began by laying out the current rules of engagement:

> We're going to have to get much better at if we want to engage people. Number one is dramatically reducing the level of fear in organizations. Number two is depoliticizing decision making so people don't feel that decisions are basically a function of political power and access but really a function of good ideas; creating a democracy of information where you have complete transparency and people don't hold information, don't use it as a political weapon, reducing the power of the traditional hierarchy; doing all kinds of things to unleash real human potential in an organization.
>
> The very sad thing, in fact, I would say it's more than sad, if you're a manager or a leader it's actually scandalous, is that despite the last 30 to 40 years where we've talked about empowerment and engagement—we no longer call employees, employees; we call them team members, associates, and so on—despite all that,

if you look at the data on employee engagement from around the world, virtually in no country are more than about 20 percent of employees truly engaged in their work by their own admission. And so you think about that as a manager and say that means that basically about 80 percent of people or 80 percent of their time, they're there physically, and that's it.

Here we are fighting through a recession, worrying about how you take the next 3 or 4 percent of costs out. By far the greatest untapped source of wealth and potential in any organization is all those people who've chosen on that particular day not to bring their imagination to work, not to bring their passion to work, not to bring their initiative to work. And the irony is, in the economy we live in today, which is not anymore a knowledge economy, knowledge is a commodity. We're now in a creative economy, and in that world the capabilities that we need most out of our employees, their imagination, initiative, and so on, are exactly the capabilities that are most difficult to command. You cannot tell somebody to show initiative or to be creative. Well, you can tell them, but it's not going to do much good. Those are things that literally are gifts that people choose to bring to work every day or they don't. And the moment you acknowledge those two things, you acknowledge first of all that the capabilities that count most today are gifts and second that they cannot be commanded.

That by itself turns management upside down because as a manager, the problem today is not, How do I get people to serve the organization; the problem is, How do I create the work environment, the sense of purpose and mission that will elicit, that literally merits, the gifts of creativity and passion and so on?

And so, yes, it's an enormous issue, I would say particularly for Western companies. Either we join the race to the bottom, everything goes offshore, and one day we're all employing Chinese prisoners or something, or we have to figure out how to get people to bring these capabilities to work every day. And that's going to require a fundamental change in the way managers see their roles, their behaviors, and so on.

The challenge of engaging employees is likely to increase as the more questioning and attractively skeptical millennials enter the workforce and take on leadership roles. There are, as yet, few suggestions that ever-bigger carrots for the senior echelons of executives are the motivational answer.

Only Engage

David MacLeod was commissioned by the British government's Department for Business to take an in-depth look at employee engagement and report on its potential benefits for organizations and employees. This led to the MacLeod Report on Employee Engagement: *Engaging for Success: Enhancing Performance Through Employee Engagement.*

It was the first report commissioned by the British government on this important topic. David MacLeod invited us to work with his team to help them articulate their findings.

Can you define employee engagement?

We've come across 56 definitions so far in this eight-month study, but if you boil it all down, it's basically, How do you unlock the potential of people at work? If people have got this much potential and they're only offering this much of it, how do we ensure that more of it is available for their benefit and for the organization's benefit?

Why does that matter?

In this study we see the most fantastic examples of organizations that are really buzzing. They're successful; the people are committed. We went to somewhere in Wales and met a woman who'd worked for the same organization for 20 years. For the first 15 it was a very distinctly average engagement organization. Then they had a change. I talked to her. She said, "I give more, I'm appreciated more." Her husband found her easier to live with! She really enjoyed it and said, "I have always started work at nine and finished at five." That has not changed, but her experience of work is different.

We saw so many examples in good organizations, small and big organizations, but they were too few. There are also very clear statistics that the majority of people are not really engaged.

But the evidence is that there's a very strong correlation between whether people are engaged, whether we have managed to unlock their potential with performance. When we look at that in the public sector, in the private sector, in local authorities, if you measure people's engagement, there is likely to be a very strong correlation with better performance; that's why it matters.

We haven't proved causality, because for causality you need two exactly paired examples, and you can't construct how that could ever happen, but if you look at all the studies of organizations that have done it, the evidence is pretty compelling.

But isn't this the wrong time for such things? Companies and people have got other things on their minds. This is a nice to have rather than a business essential.

Are people fearful of walking past opportunities for customer service and for doing things quicker, leaner, and better, or are people really engaged in coming up with ideas that will help through a recession?

Now, if we're going to get through a recession and tackle, take advantage of the upturn when it comes, we need our people engaged. We need everybody's shoulder to the wheel. We need people to do that, though, in such a way that they're not manipulated to do it. They do it because they want to do it. They do it because it's in their interest to do it, because the organization set it up in that way.

Do you find that the same things happen in all the organizations that do it well?

I'm extremely wary of offering the seven steps to engagement heaven, but there are four things that do tend to be in place in organizations that are really engaged. One is that people do have a real sense of where they're trying to get to; there's some kind of strategic narrative about the future. Second, there are engaging managers right at the front line. Those engaging managers are offering clarity about what's expected, with lots of appreciation. They're treating people as human beings with hopes, fears, and wants and things they like and don't like and are trying to work with them as human beings.

Third, they're also organizing work efficiently. It's very hard to be engaged if work is very badly organized. We've also found that there's a real sense of voice in the organization. What people think moves from the front line right up to the top. I was at a conference the other day, and the chief executive was on the podium saying, "I have an open door policy," and the person next to me whispered, "Yes, open door for good news." Now, the question is whether real information, good and bad, is flowing through the organization from outside, from the customers. That's a real sense of voice.

Fourth, most organizations say they have values, and all have behavioral norms. Now, if there's a gap between the values that are espoused and what happens, that gap leads to distrust. If you bring it together, you get trust and you get integrity in the organization.

We've seen these four things in place in the most engaged organizations we've found; there's a real sense of where we're going, a real sense of an engaging manager, a voice that permeates the organization, and the values and the behaviors are together leading to trust.

Cynics might suggest that what you're saying is nothing more commonsensical than that if you treat people nicely, they'll do better work.

I think that's a very fair point to make. But if you look back at some of the antecedents—commitment and empowerment and so on—employee engagement has echoes of all these things, but the thing that makes engagement different is that it's not about the people with all the decorations on the shoulder manipulating those at the front line. True engagement is about really listening to those in the front line, really creating conditions in which those at the front line want to offer that discretionary effort so that the person in the organization benefits and the organization benefits. It's a real two-way street engagement.

CHAPTER 4

Managing Processes

The moving assembly line was tried out at Ford's Highland Park plant in April 1913. The initial experiment involved the production of the flywheel magneto, which previously had been made by a single worker. Working alone, the worker could produce between 35 and 40 pieces in a nine-hour day, with each magneto taking around 20 minutes. Ford, in Tayloristic fashion, identified 29 separate operations in the assembly process. Introducing an assembly line in which each operation was handled by a different worker reduced the assembly time to 13 minutes and 10 seconds. Then Ford raised the height of the line eight inches and cut the time to seven minutes. Further experimenting with the speed of the line cut it down to five minutes.

"In short, the result is this: by the aid of scientific study one man is now able to do somewhat more than four did only a comparatively few years ago," wrote Ford. "That line established the efficiency of the method and we now use it everywhere. The assembling of the motor, formerly done by one man, is now divided into eighty-four operations—those men do the work that three times their number formerly did."[1]

After a great deal of tinkering by Ford and his engineers, the assembly line began working. Around it Ford created a complex series of production systems that ensured that parts, subassemblies, and assemblies were delivered at the right time to the line. Ford was practicing just-in-time techniques long before they were made popular in the 1980s.

Ford brought process, rigor, and the latest technology to create mass production. That approach helped create the American industrial colossus. By the time of World War II, American mastery of the production process was at its zenith. Sheer industrial capacity helped win the war.

Japan watched and learned. In August 1946 Japan's Federation of Economic Organizations (FEO) was created. It became one of the mainsprings of Japanese economic renewal, with over 750 large corporations and 100 major national trade associations. FEO was the power behind the revival of Japan Inc. and announced its main purpose as "to maintain close contact with all sectors of the business community for the purpose of adjusting and harmonizing conflicting views and interests of the various businesses and industries represented in its huge membership. It is the front office of the business community and is in effect a partner of the government." FEO's first president was Ichiro Ishikawa, a successful industrialist who was also president of the Japan Union of Scientists and Engineers (JUSE), that nation's most important quality control organization, founded in 1946.

The next move forward came when Ishikawa invited a census bureau statistician named W. Edwards Deming (1900–1993) to give a lecture to Tokyo's Industry Club in July 1950. Deming had first visited Japan in 1947 to aid in the development of what was to become the 1951 census. His message was different from the usual quality control theory in that he emphasized the deficiencies of management. If quality was to happen, it had to be led by management. The new generation had to seize the day.

"I did not just talk about quality. I explained to management their responsibilities," Deming recalled. "Management of Japan went into action, knowing something about their responsibilities and learning more about their responsibilities."[2] Japan embraced Deming and his ideas, and they played a major role in that country's economic recovery.

It was only in the 1980s that the West stumbled upon Deming's work (via an NBC television program). Slow off the blocks, it sought to catch up. Before long Total Quality Management (TQM) and a range of other tools were being practiced by corporations throughout the Western world.

Reengineering Work

In the 1990s the process side of business came to dominate under the title of reengineering. Reengineering was the business idea of the early 1990s. It was brought to the fore by the American management consultants James Champy, cofounder of the consultancy CSC Index, and Michael Hammer (1948–2008), an electrical engineer and former computer science professor at MIT.

Champy and Hammer's book *Reengineering the Corporation* was a bestseller that produced a plethora of reengineering programs, the creation of many consulting companies, and a deluge of books promoting alternative approaches to reengineering. Thanks to the popularity of reengineering, CSC also became one of the largest consulting firms in the world.

The fundamental idea behind reengineering was that organizations needed to identify their key processes and make them as lean and efficient as possible. Peripheral processes (and, therefore, peripheral people) had to be discarded. "Don't automate; obliterate," said Hammer. A wave of downsizing followed as corporations throughout the world obliterated in the name of reengineering.

The lessons from reengineering are many and varied. First, theorizing is one thing and practice is another. The concept of reengineering is simple; turning it into reality was immensely more difficult than its proponents suggested. The blank piece of paper on which companies were supposed to remap themselves ignored the years, often decades, of cultural evolution that led to an organization doing something in a certain way. Such preconceptions and often justifiable habits were not easily discarded.

The second lesson from reengineering is that businesses really are about people. If companies ride roughshod over people, they lose their trust and goodwill. Reengineering appeared inhumane. Significantly, when the phrase was invented in 1987, *transformation* was dismissed as an alternative because it was too "touchy-feely."

The third lesson is that corporations were not—and still aren't—natural or even willing revolutionaries. Instead of casting the reengineering net widely, managers tended to reengineer the most readily accessible process and leave it at that. Related to this—and the subject of Champy's sequel, *Reengineering Management*—reengineering usually was not applied to management. Not surprisingly, managers were all too willing to impose the rigors of a process-based view of the business on others but often unwilling to inflict it on themselves. In retrospect, the mistake of reengineering was that it didn't recommend tackling management first.

We talked with Jim Champy when the reengineering movement was still in full swing but facing increasing questioning.

Reengineering is often seen as ambition gone haywire, especially by the general public.
That is because the reengineer's motivations are too often simply assumed. As change agents, we don't have to talk openly about our ambition, but we should examine it carefully. We should look at the quality of our ambition: For what purpose do we strive? Is there a "greater" purpose in what we do beyond just generating profits? Too often we experience the ambition of others as overreaching and failure. Most people talk and write about ambition in that way. Sometimes well-intentioned people get to a point where they believe themselves infallible and do foolish things.

Has the reengineering movement been positive?
I think that the balance is very positive. In global terms, I think that we have only reached 10 or 20 percent of what we intended, so there is still a lot to be done. In this moment there is a very real reaction

to reengineering that comes from people who do not understand the concept. Many consider it very similar to the downsizing trend. Others have not yet understood the need for a fundamental change in the way in which corporations work. Reengineering is exactly that—it is a radical change in the way people perform their work in corporations. The basic idea of reengineering is now a global phenomenon. More than a management fad and a buzzword, it is really a genuine need.

Which sectors of the economy had the best results?

I am not sure that there is a clear answer to your question. I can name those industries that in my opinion should urgently start reengineering projects. In the first place are the industries linked with technologies, the telecommunications and media enterprises. Your business press, for example, is a strong candidate for reengineering because your industries are making a revolution in the history of information and of publications. In the second place are the financial services, the banks in particular, whose reengineering isn't done yet. Then there are the health services. In the United States maybe more than in Europe, the health system is experiencing important changes. It is also important to note the public utilities that live in a phase of deregulation and privatization around the world. Last are the transportation industries, which stand to reap great benefits from reengineering that currently are being lost.

Were there reengineering differences between
Europe, the United States, and Asia?

In cultural terms, I think that North American managers are better prepared to be radical and to cut
their ties with the past. In Europe, generally, managers are more conservative. Some countries, such as
France, are heavily influenced by socialist traditions.
But in Germany, there is recognition of the necessity
of applying reengineering. Germany is one of the better markets nowadays to apply the concept. Although
the Germans are conservative, they are very much
aware of the need for change, particularly in the
automobile sector. In Asia, I have seen reengineering
in locations such as South Korea, Japan, and Hong
Kong. Among these, the Japanese are the ones who
show more willingness to try to do things differently.

Why the Japanese?

The Japanese are facing a great challenge because
they are not moving as fast as their competitors in
the management of change. That is one of the motivations for Japanese corporations to build new plants
outside Japan. Change is easier to implement because
the culture is less resistant. With the Koreans the situation is different. They are more open to foreign
ideas and ways of thinking. The Chinese, on the other
side, still do not have reengineering infrastructures in
place, because their businesses are like collections of
small operations. In spite of everything, they seem to
be facing the change well.

How will the dramatic changes you talk about manage to take place?

Without being ironic, I think that each corporation needs a shrink. My work is to persuade the manager to see the market in a different way, to understand the level of change that is adequate, and to agree about the necessity of making changes in how work is done. That is without any doubt the most difficult part. I think that the techniques related to process redesign are easy to understand and implement. Those linked with great cultural changes are more complicated. That is due to the fact that the managers still have, in my opinion, a traditional way of thinking. The change I talk about is radical and discontinuous, not incremental, contrary to what we are used to daily.

Are consultants required to implement reengineering?

Companies will probably learn to do it by themselves, but in my opinion, not with the greatest change efforts. Companies still do not know how to change strategy, the processes, the technology, and the culture simultaneously without external help. It will still take 10 years until the muscle of management will be able to do it. The reengineering movement still has to go through all the steps that strategy has already passed. Ten years ago, the best consultant companies that specialized in strategy were growing at a good pace: McKinsey, Boston Consulting Group, Bain and Monitor, Michael Porter. On a large scale that business decreased due to the fact that managers have learned to develop that discipline. Nowadays people know that the way to a good performance doesn't lie only in having a brilliant idea or strategy but also in looking at the processes. I think that the consulting firms still have about 5 to 10 good years of reengineering work. After that, it is probable that there will be a new phase of accommodation.

How long is a reengineering journey?
In my opinion, the complete journey takes two to three years. But there should be concrete results in the first 12 or 18 months or the resistance to reengineering will certainly grow.

And to counter that resistance?
Many people don't understand the subtleties of managing. They believe that a manager must be decisive, that the world is black and white. In fact, a good bit of the business world today is gray; you may not know immediately what to do. It's okay to think for a while. There is a lot of intellectual work to management, but that counters the macho approach that mangers often adopt to maintain power. Operating only through control diminishes your power to lead people. It suggests that you really don't know what's going on.

High Velocity

More recently, a fresh take on quality and how exceptional organizations can create competitive advantage through the strength of their internal operations has come from Steven Spear, senior lecturer at MIT and author of *The High-Velocity Edge*. We asked Spear some quick questions.

How would you describe what you label a high-velocity organization?

I write about companies succeeding over many years, sometimes decades, in even the most hypercompetitive markets. Given the intense rivalry in these markets, no one should get a lead, and if they do, then others should overtake them. But these high-velocity companies, as people start to close the gap, come up with another good idea about what the market needs, what to offer the market, and how to deliver it, and they keep running away. So they're the firms setting the pace, leaving it to everyone else to try to catch up.

Can you name some of the high-velocity organizations you looked at in your research?

When I first started my research, I looked at Toyota. Toyota not only maintained a lead over its rivals, it widened the lead. It kept advancing quality and productivity, entered new regions, expanded its product portfolio by adding new brands such as Lexus, and at the time was on the cusp of introducing new technology such as the Prius hybrid. It just kept running away from the field.

Other companies that had continued to create and then widen a gap in hypercompetitive markets included Southwest Airlines in commercial aviation in the United States and Alcoa in heavy industry.

You spent some time at a Toyota supplier in the United States. What did you discover?
Toyota realized a long time ago that it has these very, very complex systems. The car is complex, the equipment to make the car is complex, the factory is complex, the supply network is complex.

And it kept discovering that as much as it invested in trying to design these complex systems, it designed very imperfect systems. But there was discovery over time where it realized that if it couldn't design perfect systems, it had to constantly, relentlessly discover perfection.

If you can't see the subtlety, the nuance, and the details of how work gets done, you're likely to miss opportunities to get better. But if you really train yourself, starting with what's going on in the truck and then working your way to much more sophisticated situations, more nuanced situations, you have a chance to gain insight and convert what you don't understand into knowledge which is useful.

Are there some characteristics and universal principles that apply across the board?
Sure. It's rooted in the problem people have, particularly when working in large groups, that no matter how smart they are, how much effort they invest,

they're going to design something complex and it's going to be broken. The problem is that they just don't know how.

The folks at these high-velocity organizations are optimistic, though, in the sense that they believe that if they can see the problems and see them quickly, they can solve those problems. So the very first capability or principle here is that work is designed in these high-velocity organizations so that the problems are immediately evident when and where they occur.

Anything else?

The second capability is that when problems present themselves, these organizations don't just say that's normal, it always happens, and then work around the problem: cope and compensate.

When they see problems, they swarm them very aggressively and with tremendous discipline; they understand the root cause of the problem, develop a treatment, and then follow up to make sure the treatment works. And if it does, they realize they've converted something they didn't understand—that's why they had the problem—into something they do understand.

How do you use that knowledge for the organization's benefit?

Once they've got this little pocket of knowledge, the most sophisticated organizations realize that if you've had ignorance in one place, you probably have the same ignorance laced throughout your system. If you can get a multiplier effect by spreading what's learned locally in a disciplined fashion and make it systemically useful, then you get this huge return on your investment in solving the problem.

So the third capability of these high-velocity organizations is tremendous discipline around knowledge sharing.

What about leadership in this context?
Well, the fourth capability is leadership. The conventional wisdom on what leaders do is that they make decisions, they delegate other decisions, they give commands, they enforce them, and they ensure compliance.

But at Toyota when I asked people to tell me about the best leader they ever had, every single person told me a story about a leader they had at some point who took the time and effort to teach them how to be a great learner in their right and how to teach others to do the same.

So this different style of leadership also sets the high-velocity organizations apart.
That's right. People say, What's difficult about this? The tools are not the hard part. There are hundreds if not thousands of people who can sell you the tools. The hard part is the leadership model.

With high-velocity organizations, the whole operating system is based on the premise that the job of a leader is to find ignorance, convert it to knowledge, and teach others to do the same. So to convert a company from a typical company into a high-velocity one fundamentally demands that leaders change their posture and their approach from telling other people what to do to helping other people discover it and, when in doubt, leading the way on discovery.

And the thing about leading the way on discovery is that the very first step is raising your hand and saying, I just don't understand.

Toyota has become extraordinarily successful based on a model of developing people to be very agile learners, so that the products and the processes got much better more quickly than anyone else in the industry could manage.

That development of people depends on a very intimate coaching process, and that coaching process had more and more demands placed on it as Toyota's business expanded through the 1980s and 1990s. The real challenge is maintaining the intimacy and continuity of those coaching-mentor-apprenticeship relationships and developing enough people fast enough.

Of course, sleek and effective processes and quality products and services require constant attention and commitment. For example, over recent years, Toyota has had its troubles. The point remains valid, probably even more so given the rise of competition, especially in manufacturing, from China and elsewhere. Processes must be managed and maximized. To fail to do so is to fail.

CHAPTER 5

Measuring
Performance

What's measured gets done. Nowhere is this truer than in management. But what to measure? As we have seen, what managers do is cloaked in uncertainty and ambiguity. Financial measures are clearly vital but are only part of the story. In the 1990s, at the opposite extreme it was argued that intellectual capital should be considered the vital measure of corporate health. More recently, debates continue on social value as a key measure.

To take companies beyond the often limiting measurement of financial criteria, David Norton and Robert Kaplan developed the *balanced scorecard*, "a strategic management and measurement system that links strategic objectives to comprehensive indicators." Norton is a cofounder of the consulting company

Renaissance Solutions, and Kaplan is Marvin Bower Professor of Leadership Development at Harvard Business School. The duo developed the balanced scorecard concept at the beginning of the 1990s in research sponsored by KPMG.

The result was an article in the *Harvard Business Review* ("The Balanced Scorecard," January/February 1993). The article had a simple message for managers: what you measure is what you get. Norton and Kaplan compared running a company to flying a plane: a pilot who relies on a single dial is unlikely to be safe. Pilots must utilize all the information contained in their cockpits. "The complexity of managing an organization today requires that managers be able to view performance in several areas simultaneously," said Norton and Kaplan. "Moreover, by forcing senior managers to consider all the important operational measures together, the balanced scorecard can let them see whether improvement in one area may be achieved at the expense of another."

Norton and Kaplan suggest that four elements need to be balanced: the customer perspective—companies need to ask how customers perceive them; the internal perspective—companies need to ask what is it that they must excel at; the innovation and learning perspective—companies must ask how they can improve and create value; and the financial perspective—a company has to ask how its shareholders perceive it.

According to Norton and Kaplan, by focusing energy, attention, and measures on all four of these dimensions, companies become driven by their mission rather than by short-term financial performance. Applying measures to company strategy is crucial to achieving this goal. Instead of being beyond measurement, strategy, according to the balanced scorecard, must be central to any process of scorecard measurement: "A good balanced scorecard should tell the story of your strategy."

Identifying the essential measures for an organization is not straightforward. One company produced 500 measures on its first examination; this was distilled down to a 7-measure scorecard (20 is par for the course). According to Norton and Kaplan, a good balanced scorecard contains three elements. First, it establishes cause-and-effect relationships: rather than being isolated figures, measures are related to one another and the network of relationships makes up the strategy. Second, a balanced scorecard should have a combination of lead and lag indicators. Lag indicators are measures, such as market share, that are common across an industry and, though important, offer no distinctive advantage. Lead indicators are measures that are company- and strategy-specific. Third, an effective balanced scorecard is linked to financial measures. By this, Norton and Kaplan mean that initiatives such as reengineering and lean production need to be tied to financial measures rather than pursued indiscriminately.

In many ways, the concept of the balanced scorecard is brazen but welcome common sense. Balance is clearly preferable to imbalance. (The counterintuitive reality is that unbalanced companies, usually driven by a single dominant individual, have often been short-term successes.) The balanced scorecard is now widely championed by a variety of companies. Indeed, it has, somewhat ironically, become a management fad. Its argument that blind faith in a single measurement or a small range of measures is dangerous is a powerful one. However, effective measures of elements, such as management competencies and intellectual capital, remain elusive.

Keeping Score

The balanced scorecard spawned an industry. Kaplan and Norton's books—*The Balanced Scorecard*, *The Strategy-Focused Organization*, *Strategy Maps*, and *Alignment*—are bestsellers. The Balanced Scorecard Collaborative, a group of professional service firms that helps companies use the balanced scorecard, has offices and affiliates throughout the world. There is even a Balanced Scorecard Hall of Fame. We talked with the concept's cocreator, David Norton.

Can you give us an overview of the balanced scorecard?

At the heart is the idea that organizations don't have systems to manage strategy. This is primarily because they don't have a framework to describe a strategy. What we've been able to do with the balanced scorecard is to solve that first problem of how you describe the strategy of an organization. Our book *The Strategy Map* gives the way to describe a strategy, and then *The Balanced Scorecard* is about translating that into a measurement scheme. And then the third book, *The Strategy-Focused Organization*, says, take the measurement scheme and tie it to the way you manage your organization, tie it to your budgets, tie it to your people's objectives, tie it to their compensation, and align these things around the strategy.

So *alignment* is an important piece of the system for managing strategy. The big issue that sits underneath the book has to do with organization design. If you go back to the classical business school theory of strategy and structure, the argument is that structure follows strategy. Then, in 2000, we got a new economy forming that was structurally at odds with what we had had. Outsourcing, intellectual capital, being customer-centric, and all of these things basically require different kinds of structures.

Structure is probably the biggest impediment to change. You can't get an organization to reorganize just to execute a strategy. But we have 60-odd companies in our hall of fame that have executed their strategies and used the balanced scorecard approach, and very few of them reorganized in order to pull this off. Bob Kaplan and I started pondering why, if structure follows strategy, they aren't reorganizing.

And the answer is?

They're accepting the organization as it exists, because there are reasons why it exists and there's a lot of good in it. Rather than playing with the structure, they're playing with the system. They're defining a planning process that cuts across the organization; they're defining incentive compensation that cuts across the organization. So everything about strategy management that we have observed in these successful companies and written about basically is a way to cut across the traditional power structures, to cut across the silos. Alignment is really the organization approach: How do you execute strategy without reorganizing?

The balanced scorecard has been hugely successful internationally. Does that ever surprise you?

Of course if somebody described the way this has turned out, you'd really be surprised. My rule of thumb is to never look back, keep looking forward. Very few ideas catch on, so you look at it and say, Why? You've got to depersonalize it. What is it about this idea? And I think that if an idea is going to have staying power, it has to be an idea that's at the right time and the right place. The right time was the new economy that made the measurement and management systems that we were using somewhat obsolete because they were siloed and hierarchical when the new economy required you to be holistic and cross-functional.

So there was a need, and then the right place was the measurement system. The tool that all managers use to organize their performance management program is the measurement framework they put in place. Those two things came together, and we came up with the idea of balancing financial and nonfinancial indicators.

The idea is commonsensical once you've heard it.

Yes. As somebody once said, common sense isn't all that common. And of course, the phrase was just right. *Balance* and *scorecard* just hit it right, said what it was. But I think what made it stick was the thinking underneath it. When it was first written, the idea of balance was, well, there's four things, and only one of them is financial. Another level of thinking has subsequently come to the fore, and that is a cause-and-effect relationship among those four things. What it is really describing is how you create value.

Happy customers lead to happy shareholders. Then the question was, Well, how do I please my customers? Well, you do it through processes, you do research and build better products, you service them better, and so forth. And then, finally, Well, how do I get better processes? Well, that's built on the skills of my people and confidence in the climate. A sound climate leads to good processes, which lead to happy customers and then to happy shareholders. This cause-and-effect model really has stood out over time. Companies are able to describe their strategies, which they couldn't do before. They were trying to manage strategies but were unable to describe them; it's like shooting in the dark.

Who came up with the phrase the balanced scorecard?

Bob Kaplan and I had this research group that we were leading, and it started with the objective of finding a better way to manage. U.S. companies in particular and Western companies in general were getting beaten badly by the Japanese, and there was a lot being written about short-term America and how we were doing it to ourselves with this quarterly focus on financials. That was the front-of-mind problem. We were looking for a better way. Our first conclusion was that you can't throw away the financials—that is the lifeblood—but you've got to somehow make it long term as well as short term. *Balancing* just came naturally to describe that. We're balancing long term and short term, we're balancing lead indicators with lag indicators, and so it was a natural outcome. I can't remember seeing a flash of light, and it didn't happen in the shower in the morning.

What about the international responses to the balanced scorecard? When you took it out on the road and introduced people to it, did the reactions vary from continent to continent?

Bain does this survey of the tools that managers use. The most recent one says that in the United States and Western Europe, about 60 percent of companies use a balanced scorecard. I think for Latin America it is something like 40 percent or so, and in Asia about a third of companies claim to be using it. So there's been a lag internationally. Now we have this Balanced Scorecard Hall of Fame with 70 companies in there, and they come from every corner of the world.

There are some cultural assumptions that we've built into our approach, for example, that strategy is everyone's job, that you should push strategy down to the front lines in the workforce. I had some questions about how this would go down in, let's say, Western Europe, where labor unions are stronger. Or how would it work in the more hierarchical societies in Latin America? What we found is that the approach is flexible enough to adapt to cultural differences. So if your approach is make strategy everyone's job, well, it doesn't tell you how to do that; it just says it's important to bring the workforce into the process.

I can remember talking in South Africa, and somebody put her hand up and said, "I don't know how that will work here in South Africa, because in my company 40 percent of the workforce is illiterate. How can we educate them on the strategy if they're illiterate?" And before I stammered a reply, somebody put his hand up and said, "Look, we have used this approach here in our company, and we have the same issue—40 percent are illiterate—but that doesn't mean you can't communicate to people. We always communicate to them, we communicate to them about safety and about work habits, and so forth; you just have to select the media. You can't use traditional reading and writing as the way to communicate, but you can communicate, and we found it a significant payoff by being open and explaining to people what you're trying to do and the directions you're going."

So they adapted it. It wouldn't be the approach we would have used with the glossy brochures that many companies use whether in Japan or here, but they communicated the strategy to everyone in the organization.

When you see a statistic like 60 percent of companies are using the balanced scorecard, what's your

*reaction? Are you deeply worried by this? Say 60
percent are. In all likelihood, among those companies,
80 percent are doing so in a haphazard way you
wouldn't approve of, we suspect.*

Exactly. Another estimate is that 50 percent are doing
it wrong. When we say the balanced scorecard, we
mean a system for managing strategy which uses the
balanced scorecard as the organizing framework.
Fifty percent or so of the companies that say they're
using a balanced scorecard are trying to do that, but
50 percent are doing it in some other way. My worst
nightmare is that I'm going to wake up some day
and see an article that says 70 percent of balanced
scorecard users fail, because that's what happened to
reengineering.

*With reengineering, they said at one point that 80
percent of American companies were using it.*

That's right. Reengineering started out with a sound
basis. It had to do with restructuring, a process rather
than a functional view of companies. But then you
started seeing reports that reengineering was failing.
When somebody said reengineering was failing, no
one was able to step in and say, This isn't reengineering; this is something else.

One of the things we have done with the balanced scorecard as a brand is that we have sought to
defend it by moving it forward, by basically maintaining the association with our own names, Kaplan and
Norton, so first of all it becomes synonymous, and

then building an organization that is able to execute on the balanced scorecard the right way. That also allows us to learn from our clients what the right way is. So it's a two-way street. You need to have that consulting organization, and you need to keep the idea moving forward.

I think with reengineering they wrote the book and were probably overwhelmed by the response. With the balanced scorecard we started with the measurement framework, and then, as we began to see how organizations used it to manage strategy, we saw it was bigger than a measurement framework; it was a management system.

I think we did some good work around human capital and measuring its role in organizations, and then alignment and strategy maps were all builds on the original idea. They have allowed us to keep pushing it forward, making it more flexible, taking it into niches, and at the same time building a body of knowledge around it. The Balanced Scorecard Hall of Fame is why I sleep well at night. I don't have that nightmare of a quote in a magazine saying 75 percent of organizations do it wrong. In the hall of fame, although I don't know what percentage they represent, there are over 60 companies that did it right.

They officially validate your idea.
That's right. So no matter how many people fail, if I've got 60 companies from around the world, every industry, every niche, in the public sector, the private

sector, that have done it successfully, then the message is clear. You can do it successfully if you know how.

How is it used differently in the public sector?

The primary difference is the payoff. In the private sector the payoff is financial; it's return on investment for the shareholders, the ultimate point of accountability. In the public sector, organizations are mission-focused. For example, the Department of Commerce in the United States is the economic development agency. Its mission is to invest in the economic development of distressed communities, either poor communities or communities that have had disasters. For the American Diabetes Association the mission is to improve the life and hopes of victims and potential victims of diabetes. Its payoff is reducing the incidence of diabetes, extending the life of people who do have the disease, and so forth.

It is the highest-level objective that's different, but once you establish that strategy is strategy, you've got processes, you've got customers, you've got people, you've got technology, and you've got to put those all to work to achieve that high-level objective. It is just the same thing they do in a private sector company.

So there's probably quite a lot of room for growth of the concept in the public sector?

In many ways the idea is better suited for the public sector in the sense that in the private sector you could probably get a little sloppy and still not lose control of your organization, because ultimately the financial discipline will force you to get back together again. You're always accountable to the shareholders. In the public sector you generally don't have competition, but if you clarify your mission and then tie it to measures that drive the actions of your organization, this is very powerful.

The new discipline is to ask, How do I measure whether I'm achieving my mission? This really forces you to think this through. The language of measurement is very powerful here. If your job is to improve the lot of people who are susceptible to diabetes, how would you know whether you're succeeding? How would you know that all the money you've raised from donors is being well applied? There are other diabetes associations, so maybe you can learn from others, but it's not like being in consumer banking, where you've got all kinds of points of reference, best practices, and things like that available to you.

Companies are still criticized for their short-termism and overly emphasizing shareholder value, so in many ways the things that instigated you or your thinking in the early 1990s actually still apply.

Yes, the quarterly report is still the life cycle in organizations, particularly in the United States, and so the battle isn't won at all yet. I talked to several executives when we went through the downturn in 2000–2002. When the bubble burst, there were a lot of organizations that were suddenly off the growth path, back in survival mode and cutting costs. I asked these CEOs, Did you throw out the balanced scorecard when you had to cut costs? Is the balanced scorecard just a growth tool? Their response was pleasantly surprising. They said there are forces outside of their control pushing on them. The board of directors, for example, wants to see a coherent program to reduce costs. Now, if they didn't have the balanced scorecard, essentially what they would do is go through budget-line items and everything that's discretionary would be cut, including half of the initiatives that are required for their long-term strategy. I think it's proved flexible enough to allow an organization to remain balanced even when there are short-term pressures.

In 10 years where do you see the balanced scorecard?

I have a crystal-clear vision of where it could go. I use the quality movement as my point of reference. When you think of quality and ideas like that, these are ideas that move through a system; they move through the society, and it takes 25, 30 years or so. Quality is most analogous because it's an idea that has statistical foundations and created a competitive advantage for companies that mastered it, and ultimately, it became a discipline in organizations that required special knowledge, certification, and so forth, and leadership at the executive levels of organizations. So I see a lot of parallels to the balanced scorecard in strategy management. It's an idea, at the right time and in the right place; it's creating competitive advantages for organizations; and it's not easy to manage strategy—9 out of 10 organizations fail to do it—so almost by definition you have a competitive advantage.

This means that organizations need to pay attention to this because like quality, it does give you an advantage, and it can be learned. In studying these successful companies, we've seen that they use common management practices, and we've chronicled many of them. And so it can be learned if you set out to do it, just like quality. Somewhere down the line I would love to be able to certify that these people have black belts in strategy management because they do these things. Then I'll never see that article about 70 percent failing because we'll know that this set of people, whatever we call them, strategy management professionals, perhaps, have been certified in an approach that we know works. And then at least we're talking about the same phenomenon.

So I think that I can see us being 70 percent of the way there now. We're seeing this idea of the office of strategy management emerge; we're seeing the discipline and the groups of people within organizations come together that have mastered these disciplines. Our goal is to continue building this capability, and our objective as an organization is to help companies build the competencies themselves; as opposed to being a consultant that does it for you, we do it with you but with the stated goal of having a very well-defined competency in your organization, so that strategy management will survive the current leader and just become a standard way of managing a business.

I think there are lot of forces that we'll see coming together over the next three to five years that might end up with this looking very much like the quality movement. Logic says you have to manage strategy. Everybody has a strategy. The job of those at the top is to execute the strategy, and if they don't execute the strategy, they shouldn't have the job. But there is no process to manage it, and that awareness hasn't dawned on a lot of executives because they never had it, and so they can't miss it. Our job is to bring that message to the world.

We talked to David Norton in 2006. The world has moved on, but the balanced scorecard has retained its popularity. Its attractions are that it is accessible, is easy to communicate, and is positioned as a supporting tool for managers rather than a cure for all known managerial ills. It is a triumph of pragmatism with rigor.

CHAPTER 6

Managing Change

Change is a fact of managerial life. Organizations change. Markets change. Leaders change. Contexts change. Technologies change. There is nothing new in this. Perhaps one of the biggest conceits of our time is the belief that our age is characterized by change at an unprecedented level. Change is the default setting of managerial life and of life itself. Everyone in a managerial or leadership role is involved with change.

MIT's Edgar Schein believes that organizational culture evolves through a number of distinctive stages and that each stage requires a different type of leadership. For Schein, effective leadership does not depend so much on the individual activities a leader encounters during the day as it does on which stage of its life cycle an organization has reached. For each stage of organizational evolution there is a different corresponding leadership role: creating, building, maintaining, and changing.

In the creating stage, the entrepreneurial leader tries to get the organization off the ground. In doing this, as they wrestle with funding issues, try out different ideas, and inspire and enthuse their followers, these leaders demonstrate high levels of energy. Schein calls this stage, typified by the leader's vibrant and energetic approach, *the leader as animator.*

When the organization has gained enough traction to be viable, the leader imprints his or her beliefs and values on the followers. Leaders do this by hiring like-minded people, indoctrinating employees in their way of thinking, and acting as role models for their followers. At this point, says Schein, if the organization is successful and that success is associated with the leader, the leader's personality becomes part of the corporate culture. At the same time, if the leader is conflicted, wanting collaboration but also wanting control, for example, those conflicts will be locked into the culture. At this evolutionary stage the leader is *the creator of culture.*

The third life cycle stage is maintaining. When organizations outgrow their youthful exuberance and mature, a different set of challenges emerge: commoditization of products, a changing and growing workforce, more intense competition, and greater complexity. Entrepreneurial leaders often struggle at this point. The leaders who succeed are the ones who can identify the successful aspects of the business and focus attention on them. At the same time they are able to scale up the processes that proved so successful when the company was small and fast-growing. For the leader as *a sustainer of culture*, judgment and wisdom are the most important qualities, says Schein.

Finally, Schein discusses change, paving the way for the leadership academics who have concentrated on change leadership: the leader's role in navigating change successfully. The last evolutionary stage of the organization is changing. During this phase of organizational life the leader operates as a *change agent*. When the external environment changes sufficiently, the strengths of the organization that were institutionalized during the sustaining period to ensure long-term success require changing and undoing. The challenge for the leader is not only to bring in new things but to unlearn old things that no longer work.

For leaders to be able to lead organizations through such a period of change, says Schein, they must have "the emotional strength to be supportive of the organization while it deals with the anxieties attendant upon unlearning processes that were previously successful," and they also need "a true understanding of cultural dynamics and the properties of their own organizational culture."[1]

A change agent leader cannot change the culture merely by trying to eliminate the areas that are no longer required or that are dysfunctional, argues Schein. Instead, the leader must "evolve culture by building on its strengths while letting its weaknesses atrophy over time."[2]

Pronouncements of change, change programs, and projects will not do, either. The leader has to embody the changes required, has to lead by example. The leader is transformed along with the organization. If the culture is too entrenched in the ranks of senior executives or elsewhere in the organization, the leader may have to implement a turnaround. Turnaround leaders often have to clear out the old. Layers of management go, taking their outmoded, redundant, unproductive cultural values and beliefs with them. Organizations are deconstructed and rebuilt. The old culture is destroyed while the leader establishes the conditions to create the new cultural elements of the organization.

Change is particularly challenging and requires a broad set of skills. As Schein notes: "It is more correct to think of this point in the organization's history as a time when the organization-building cycle starts afresh. Turnaround managers can then be thought of as needing many of the same qualities as entrepreneurs, particularly the ability to animate a new organization. In addition, however, a turnaround manager must deal with the anxiety and depression of the employees who remain and who feel guilty that they survived while many of their colleagues and friends did not. Rebuilding their motivation and commitment often requires higher levels of animation than does building an organization in the first place."[3]

Kotter on Change

One of the most influential people in the field of change leadership is John Kotter, Konosuke Matsushita Professor of Leadership, Emeritus at Harvard Business School.

Kotter is a graduate of MIT and Harvard, having joined the Harvard Business School faculty in 1972 as one of the youngest faculty members to be given tenure and a full professorship. He has described his chosen field as "managerial behavior."

Kotter identified eight errors to be avoided in leading an organization through change. Each error is tied to one of a series of phases that most change processes go through.

The first potential pitfall is not creating a sufficient sense of the urgent need for change. After the discovery of important drivers of change, whether that is poor performance, greater competition, or new opportunities, the information that underpins the need to change must be communicated rapidly, broadly, and with impact.

Successful change requires the efforts of a critical mass of key individuals in order to move the organization in significantly different directions. Getting that critical mass requires a sense of urgency.

This is one of the most challenging pitfalls, says Kotter, with over half of the companies he studied during his research failing at this stage. There are many reasons for this, including overestimating the success of efforts to increase urgency, underestimating how difficult it can be to get people fired up for change, being paralyzed by the potential downside, and managers worrying that they will be blamed.

Successful change agents tend to get information supporting the need for change out into the open to stimulate discussion. They engineer a position in which the consequences of a no-change option look worse than choosing change. The required urgency level, says Kotter, is when "about 75 percent of a company's management is honestly convinced that business as usual is totally unacceptable."

The next pitfall is not creating a powerful enough guiding coalition. This group of individuals requires four characteristics to perform their role. They must have sufficient power to hold up the process if they are marginalized. They need a broad spectrum of expertise. Sufficient credibility is required if the group's actions and decisions are to be taken seriously. Finally, the group must contain proven leaders. No overdeveloped egos are needed.

The next three errors are united by a common thread: vision. First, the guiding coalition must create a vision: "a picture of the future that is relatively easy to communicate and appeals to customers, stockholders, and employees. A vision always goes beyond the numbers that are typically found in five-year plans. A vision says something that helps clarify the direction in which an organization needs to move."

As Kotter also notes, the vision isn't a 30-page document or a rambling 15-minute discourse. His useful rule of thumb is that if the vision cannot be "communicated to someone in five minutes or less and get a reaction that signifies both understanding and interest," the vision is not a vision that the organization is ready to move forward to the next phase with."[4]

It is not enough to have clearly defined vision, though. That vision must be communicated widely throughout the organization with a process that ensures that everyone understands and with senior executives visibly behaving in ways that support the rhetoric. Finally, obstacles to realizing the vision must be removed whether that is a narrow job description, misaligned reward systems, or intransigent executives.

Change often involves potentially demotivating events such as layoffs, plant closures, pay cuts, and other significant changes in long-standing corporate policies, values, and ways of doing business. People need to see results early on or they are unlikely to buckle up for the long haul. One way of doing this, suggests

Kotter, is to create and celebrate short-term wins. The sixth pit-fall is neglecting to address this.

"Short-term wins," says Kotter, "show progress in the direction set by the organization itself; demonstrate that the change ideas are working; increase morale among workers who may be slipping into cynicism or suffering from the fatigue that change and stress engender; give you a chance to throw a party and say thanks; and they build momentum. Short-term wins are a reason for people to stay with the program."

Because of the difficulties associated with change, there is always a risk of celebrating victory too soon. It is hard to make change stick. It is tempting to celebrate success prematurely in an effort to persuade doubters. The problem is that the change resisters, seeing an opportunity to abandon the pursuit of change, if only temporarily, are just as likely to herald the successful trans-formation. After the celebration, they will be urging everyone to pack up tools and go home, having completed the project. Thus, a potentially successful transformation is defeated at the very last moment, and the status quo and attendant traditions remerge.

It is far better, suggests Kotter, to present change as an ongoing process, with attention shifting to other points of focus, rather than a discrete exercise. Use the momentum for change and the growing expertise around the change process to lead people on to other transformations.

The last mistake associated with the phases of change is failing to institutionalize change into the culture of the organiza-tion so that it becomes "the way things are done around here." Two factors are particularly important here: demonstrably link-ing new success to new changes and making sure the talent pipe-line embodies the changes.

Change First

When we spoke with John Kotter, we began at the beginning of his personal change journey.

What got you interested in the field of change in the first place?

I've always been interested, actually, in performance, curious about why organizations, managers, and so on perform. That led me to the topic of change because the businesses mostly—but government afterward—that were performing best were dealing better in a more rapidly changing environment. So that leads to trying to understand what change is about on the outside and how they're dealing with it inside organizations.

How do you work?

The simple logic of my work is that I am a pure field guy. I hang around talking to people. I talk to managers. I sit and watch them. I snoop around, listen to their problems. It's simple detective work. My work is developed by looking out of the window at what's going on. It is about seeing patterns. If I'm good at anything, it's pattern analysis and thinking through the implications of those patterns.

I use stories constantly; 95 percent of what I do is storytelling. It has evolved as I've thought about it as a process of education.

What are your stories drawn from?

There's no one who has spent more time talking to managers. That's one reason why my books have won awards. I spend a huge amount of time talking to people.

Is that worth more than theorizing?

Who would write a better book about trees: someone in the forest or someone in an office?

You have written about change and the importance of a mobilizing, inspiring vision. Is that possible in an environment marked by downsizing?

It is not easy, but it is both possible and necessary. The key is to go beyond the downsizing clichés, talking only about lean and nice. Also, carefree statements such as "I see a smaller firm in the future" are not a vision that allows people to see a light at the end of the tunnel, that mobilizes people, or that makes them endure sacrifices.

So what's your advice?

Be creative, be genuine, and most of all, know why you're doing what you're doing. Communicate that and the organization will be stronger. Anything short of this will breed the cynicism that results when we see inconsistencies between what people say and what they do, between talk and practice.

Can a single person ignite true change?

The desire for change may start with one person: the Lee Iacocca, Sam Walton, or Lou Gerstner. But it certainly doesn't end there. Nobody can provoke great changes alone. There are people who think it is possible, but that is not true. Successful change requires the efforts of a critical mass of key individuals—a group of 2 to 50 people, depending on the size of the corporation we are considering—to move the organization in significantly different directions. If the minimum of critical mass is not reached in the first stages, nothing really important will happen.

Failing to establish a sense of urgency is one of the key mistakes made by change leaders. In Leading Change *you discuss seven additional steps in successful change efforts.*

That's right. Beyond establishing a sense of urgency, organizations need to create a powerful, guiding coalition; develop vision and strategy; communicate the change vision; empower broad-based action; celebrate short-term wins; continuously reinvigorate the initiative with new projects and participants; and anchor the change in the corporate culture.

What does this guiding coalition look like?

The guiding coalition needs to have four characteristics. First, it needs to have position power. The group needs to consist of a combination of individuals who, if left out of the process, are in positions to block progress. Second, it requires expertise. The group needs a variety of skills, perspectives, experiences, and so forth, relative to the project. Third, it needs credibility. When the group announces initiatives, will its members have reputations that get the ideas taken seriously? Fourth, it requires leadership. The group needs to be composed of proven leaders. Remember, in all of this the guiding coalition should not be assumed to be composed exclusively of managers. Leadership is found throughout the organization, and it's leadership you want, not management.

Who needs to be avoided in building this team?
Individuals with large egos and those I call snakes. The bigger the ego, the less space there is for anyone else to think and work. Snakes are individuals who destroy trust. They spread rumors, talk about other group members behind their backs, and nod yes in meetings but condemn project ideas as unworkable or shortsighted when talking with colleagues. Trust is critical in successful change efforts, and these two sorts of individuals put trust in jeopardy.

Communication *seems to crop up in most discussions of organizational effectiveness and certainly in discussions of effective change. What do you mean when you use the term?*
Effectively communicating the change vision is critical to success. This should seem obvious, yet for some reason, executives tend to stop communicating during

change when in actuality they should be communicating more than ever. Effective change communication is both verbal and nonverbal. It includes simplicity, communicating via different types of forums and over various channels, leading by example—which is very important—and two-way communication. Change is stressful for everyone. This is the worst possible time for executives to close themselves off from contact with employees. This is particularly important if short-term sacrifices are necessary, including firing people.

You came up with the rather startling statistic that 70 percent of change programs either fail or disappoint.
We've actually redone that, and there was a bigger study that said that with large-scale change, which is particularly what I'm interested in because it's becoming more and more and more important, in 70 percent of the cases, in one way or another they fail and maybe in 20 percent it's okay and 5 percent actually get it right.

Does it depress you that so many years on 70 percent are failing?
Yes, but it's not as bad as it sounds because the amount and the size of change that is coming at businesses today is so much larger and more often more complex than it was back then. So they've actually gotten better, but the problem has stayed just as far ahead of them.

In Buy-In: Saving Your Good Idea from Getting Shot Down, *you looked at getting people on board. You might think that a good idea would sell itself, but that's not the case.*

How do you figure out the good idea? How do you look, do the analysis, figure out that among the choices this is the best one? That's what education does 90 percent of the time. The implication is that that's the name of the game and once you've got the good idea, everybody will see the logic of it and it moves on from there, but in reality good ideas get shot down all the time. If you add that up, the cost to organizations and to society is huge.

You talk about four particular types of attacks on ideas. How do they work, and what do they look like?

Well, we see that there are four fundamental strategies that people use to take shots at even what is a great idea and sometimes succeed. One is confusion. A huge one is what we call death by delay. The number of good ideas that basically aren't killed immediately—that's a great idea and we'll do it next year. Well, by next year, whatever the conditions were that make it easy are gone.

This plays against the whole thing about urgency.

Absolutely. Government is the king of this. We'll set up this commission. That means the guy hates it and he knows that by the time the commission reports, which will be 14 years from now, everybody will have forgotten. The issue will be gone. Fearmongering is in some usually subtle way raising anxiety in the audience. And the last is just ridicule, at worst even character assassination.

It's almost impossible as an outsider to guess precisely what somebody's motives are, and they range all the way from a person who is really almost on your side and just trying to ask a question that'll help clarify a point to somebody who for whatever reason deeply hates it, may be jealous of you, and is—in as clever and nefarious a way as he can—trying to shoot you down. The response strategy we found that works doesn't worry about what's behind the curtain in the person's head.

We would have assumed that for each of the basic strategies there would be a different kind of response, but that's not what you find when you study it. There's basically just one way that you handle all of this that saves ideas.

It has four or five very simple components. The first is not doing what the body is programmed to do from a million years ago, which is fight or flight. Calmly be respectful of the person. Don't assume that this is a nasty person trying to do nasty things because it may not be.

The second is to do again what is counterintuitive to what we've been taught. The best responses tend to be simple, straightforward, and filled with common sense. It's amazing how powerful common sense is as opposed to going into levels of detail.

The third is remembering that you're always dealing with an audience. The audience may not even be there. We may be in a hallway, but the story of our conversation is going to go out, and you can't win over everybody. You can't get everybody to buy into something. Don't worry about it. What you're trying to do is get sufficient support and strong enough support that they'll accept the idea, and when you need their help, they feel strong enough that they'll say yes, I'll help you implement this somehow. The fourth is preparation. It never hurts, and in cases when the stakes are big, it is essential.

Who wants to have bullets come at them? You strategize how to keep the nasty people away. You roll the idea out when Harry is on vacation, you keep Sally off the e-mail list, and so forth. Invite them all in and let them attack you because a little bit of drama draws attention. All of a sudden people will start paying attention, and then you have the possibility of them actually listening to your commonsense response. Let the lions in; don't try to cage them.

Change Master

Rather mischievously, one reviewer called Rosabeth Moss Kanter "the Eartha Kitt of change management." The Harvard Business School professor, one of the 50 most powerful women in the world according to one magazine, is amused by the comparison to the husky-voiced songstress. "I suppose it is very flattering, perhaps a way of saying that I've been a sustained performer over the years rather than appearing in a flash and then disappearing." Then Kanter reflects on the comparison: "But how many people now know who she is?"

Another take on her place in the intellectual firmament comes from an introduction at a management seminar: "If Peter Drucker is the left brain and Tom Peters the right brain, Rosabeth Moss Kanter is the whole brain."

Although this sounds a little like the introduction of an overstimulated boxing emcee, there is no doubt that Kanter is intellectually formidable. Her career includes spells at Yale and Harvard Law School. She edited the *Harvard Business Review*, advises the CEOs of major multinationals, and is active in public service. Among other things, she was an economic advisor to Democrat Michael Dukakis when he ran for the U. S. presidency and served on Republican Mitt Romney's steering committee for his transition from head of the Olympics to Massachusetts governor. Kanter is also one of the founders of the consulting firm Goodmeasure and is involved in a host of other social and business activities.

She is also a woman in a man's world. Female management gurus—or thought leaders—are thin on the ground. Indeed, the only one of historical note is Mary Parker Follett, who died unheralded in 1933 and whose reputation Kanter has helped resuscitate.

Kanter's work, which includes the bestsellers *Change Masters*, *When Giants Learn to Dance*, *World Class*, and *Evolve!*, combines academic rigor with a degree of idealism not usually found in the bottom line–fixated world of management thinking. She does not consider idealism and business mutually exclusive.

Unlike some commentators, Kanter's worldview is not confined to the boardroom. Her doctoral thesis examined nineteenth-century utopian communities, including the Shakers. Such was her enthusiasm that in the early 1970s she compared IBM to a utopian culture. Trained as a sociologist, she found the business world beguiling. But rather than leaving her youthful utopian idealism behind, Kanter brought it to bear on the big management issues.

In her quest to get close to the corporate action, Kanter first tackled the narrow-minded, hierarchy-heavy corporation of the 1970s. In her 1977 book *Men and Women of the Corporation*, she effectively sounded the death knell for the traditional company. Unfortunately, as the bell tolled, the men and women of the corporation were too busy signing forms in triplicate, sending meaningless memos to one another, and jockeying for position in the ornate hierarchy to hear anything. The book was a powerful obituary, though the victim kept on breathing for a while longer (and can still be viewed gasping for breath in many places).

Then Kanter moved on to look at the perennially thorny issue of change in *The Change Masters* and innovation culture in *When Giants Learn to Dance*. Kanter's next book, *World Class*, outlined many of the issues now being aired by anticapitalist protesters. She describes it as "an activist's book." It looked at the need among companies, communities, and regions to create an infrastructure for collaboration. It suggests that globalization can be a force for good only if it is delivered at a local and regional level. In *Evolve!* she put her ideas in the context of the new economy.

Change Skills

In 1999 Kanter set out eight classic skills for leaders at any level who are engaged in change. Kanter says initially that "the most important things a leader can bring to a changing organization are passion, conviction, and confidence in others."[5]

Leaders need to be on the lookout for new trends, actively eliciting information from a range of stakeholders, including customers, partners, and employees. Kanter suggests cultivating a series of "listening posts" to help with this. She calls this skill *tuning in to the environment.* One should not tune out the bad news about the business, either.

The second skill involves challenging prevailing wisdom in the organization. Absorb information from different sources, look for the patterns in the information, and then construct new patterns. Question assumptions and find a new lens through which to view problems. Job rotations, interdisciplinary projects, and interactions outside the organization all help with kaleidoscopic thinking, as Kanter calls it.

Leaders must also communicate compelling aspirations that convey a clearly understood case for change. They build coalitions too, identifying early on in the process the key people who need to be on board to make things happen and then selling them the aspiration. This should be a limited group of key constituents.

When the coalition of key people is well established, they can be set loose on a series of experiments that roll out change in ways that will not sink the company if they fail. Meanwhile, the leader supports, guides, and motivates and makes sure the team is well resourced and protected, allowing it to get on with the change.

Kanter emphasizes that giving the team the room and resources to engage with change is not the same as abandoning it and then returning later to see if everything turned out for the best. It is in the middle of a transformation process that things so often go wrong. So it is the in-between stage in which the change leader earns a large proportion of his or her salary and other rewards.

Finally, a great change leader remembers to reward, recognize, and celebrate the accomplishments of the people involved in the change process. Make everyone a hero, says Kanter, because, as she points out: "There is no limit to how much recognition you can provide, and it is often free. Recognition brings the change cycle to its logical conclusion, but it also motivates people to attempt change again."[6]

Turning Change

Later in her career Kanter cast a critical eye on the role of the turnaround specialist.[7] Corporations such as Chrysler, IBM, and Gillette; sports teams such as the San Jose Sharks; and even countries such as South Africa have all experienced a major turnaround in their fortunes. But what kind of leader does it take to engineer such a risky and difficult endeavor? One with a unique combination of skills that make him or her ideally suited for the job, it seems.

On the basis of her studies of several turnaround situations, Kanter says that information and relationships are crucial aspects of turnaround leadership. A turnaround leader must facilitate a psychological turnaround of attitudes and behavior before a recovery can take place.

Good turnaround leaders possess the ability to extract information from an organization that enables them to appraise the situation and form a viable strategic turnaround plan. However, they must also have the necessary qualities to see that confidence is restored to the employees and team members as well as the people who deal with the organization.

There are four essential components of the turnaround process, according to Kanter: promoting dialogue, engendering respect, sparking collaboration, and inspiring initiative.

When turnaround CEOs grab the controls and wrest organizations out of the downward spiral of decline, often the first thing they do is encourage openness and free communication even if this means making management performance criteria and data freely available.

Turnaround leaders foster a culture of respect both internally among coworkers and externally between the company and its customers, other stakeholders, analysts, the media, and all the other parties who come into contact with the company.

This means moving beyond blame. Take Nelson Mandela's Truth and Reconciliation Commission in postapartheid South Africa, for example, says Kanter. Put the bad experiences behind you and move toward a better future.

Once the turnaround CEO has the company on a better course, it is time to tear down some internal barriers and rebuild collaborative partnerships. An energetic turnaround leader will invigorate innovation and banish destructive compartmentalization and negative attitudes. Finally, turnaround leaders can empower individuals to continue the revolution.

There is a caveat, says Kanter. Not all great leaders make great turnaround leaders.

Tools for Change

We have interviewed Kanter a number of times over the years. She is thoughtful, serious of purpose and intellect, but passionately driven to change things for the better.

Tell us about your research on turnarounds.

I have been doing some intensive case studies on situations in which failing organizations have been turned around and what that process involves and also what role innovation plays in turning around a failing organization. That's very timely at the moment, because this is definitely a time to turn things around rather than thinking about grand new visions.

One of my cases involves Gillette, a global company that is very well regarded but that slipped badly a few years ago and appointed a new CEO from outside the company. It's a classic general management situation that allows me to continue to think about leadership issues as well as about actions and steps to change direction. The issue of how you reverse course is very interesting. Most ideas about turnarounds focus on financial and organizational issues. I'm adding a psychological dimension: how leaders rebuild confidence when staff members are demoralized, how they open dialogue when information has been hoarded in silos, how they stimulate imagination and innovation when people feel punished for poor results. The secret of effective turnarounds is empowerment. One of the first things Greg Dyke did when he became director-general of the BBC was to empower program makers and broadcasters by increasing budgets, reducing bureaucracy, and becoming a cheerleader for creativity in all functions; these actions reversed a decline in audience share.

I have also been looking at this in terms of my interest in the digital age. Large institutions need to change because of the new technology and new ways to communicate they now have, which are presenting both demands and opportunities. The delivery of healthcare, education, and government services requires fundamentally different systemic models—getting big organizations out of self-perpetuating closed cycles into new modes that involve grassroots innovation guided by standards and accountability instead of rules and regulations that stifle change.

I am also very interested in the corporation as a social institution. I started looking in particular at the corporation's role in major world problems. There's a big debate about trade, about globalization, at the same time that corporate social responsibility has actually been growing as a movement, though perhaps not fast enough in light of the problems. So I want to see what role businesses actually play—positively or negatively—in the lives of countries, particularly developing countries, other than their own.

Do we have unrealistic expectations of our corporate and political leaders?

Yes. If the expectation is that a single leader can do it all, it is unrealistic. But it is also interesting how much a single leader *can* set in motion. In turnarounds it is quite striking how much fresh leadership can accomplish by unlocking talent and potential that was already in the organization but was stifled by rules, regulations, and bureaucracy.

In the corporate world we should have very high expectations and standards. I wish there were more corporate leaders stepping forward to address the accounting problems, not simply responding to the rules by saying they have honest numbers but instead talking about the responsibilities businesses have.

We should hope that people do more than just their job. In the corporate world it is not unrealistic to expect people to exercise leadership in terms of acting in advance of a crisis and not simply being defensive, something I hope to urge pharmaceutical industry leaders to do. But in the last decade, we created very unrealistic expectations of business leaders in terms of how quickly they could get major financial results. The expectations of speed and continuing growth—15 percent per year earnings growth, quarterly earnings increases—put pressure on companies to do it by any means they could. Some of those means did not necessarily accurately reflect the underlying strength or health of the company. So the expectations for speedy responses, speedy returns, unfettered growth, and so forth, are quite unrealistic.

In the 1990s there was a hope that business cycles had been defeated, and there was no patience because everything had to happen so fast. There were unrealistic expectations about big, bold moves. But there weren't unrealistic expectations about standards, speaking honestly about issues, and acting before being forced to act by government rules or regulations. Companies need to get ahead of the issues rather than waiting to be forced into a defensive posture. Leadership involves setting realistic but challenging expectations.

In one turnaround I have been involved with, one of the first things the new CEO did when he came in was to stress honest targets, realistic forecasts—in essence real numbers—and he was willing to pay the price for that, which was that the analysts didn't like the numbers. That was lowering expectations, not in some manipulative way so that they could be beaten, but to say that the company couldn't possibly deliver impossible performance. One of the ways leaders build confidence is to make short-term achievable promises and keep them; that encourages faith in their long-term vision.

We should expect people in positions of public trust and responsibility to rise to that trust and responsibility and to reflect the needs, desires, and interests of all their constituencies—but also to tell people the truth. We have been reduced to having to say things like leaders should tell the truth. Those are not unrealistic expectations.

People in the Western world got a little greedy and wanted and expected too much. When leaders are being pushed to promise these inflated things to get support from various stakeholders, especially the investment community, that's not a healthy situation. It's easier to exercise leadership when expectations are more realistic, but it's up to leaders to set those expectations.

Do you remain optimistic?

I always have a degree of optimism, though I think we're in a rough period in which things could get worse before they get better. This comes to one of my ultimate definitions of leadership: leadership looks at the roots causes and systems issues and not just at superficial issues. Trying to patch over a bad situation with a little cosmetic treatment is like putting lipstick on a bulldog. That's the wrong way to deal with a deteriorating situation. Right now we have the threat of terrorism, military action, and tremendous tension, and it has a dampening effect on countries and businesses that have no direct involvement. It creates fear, reduces investment, increases costs, and slows down the movement of goods and people.

Then we have the disclosure of corporate ethical lapses and mistakes, which creates crisis. A lot of people have lost a lot of money. Trust in institutions is low. If people don't have trust in the honesty and ethics of leaders, that's a problem. In addition, there is the weakness of the economy.

We can pretend everything is all right. But should we instead be looking more deeply at the entire underlying system and how we might fix it? Is there some different kind of policy, some reconfiguration, something else we could be doing? That's what leaders should be doing: taking a deeper look and offering new solutions rather than simply cosmetic responses.

Turnaround CEOs who come in and say let's cut costs but don't rethink the business model or assumptions are cosmetic and don't last. But if they come in and say we need to rethink some practices, how we are organized and the underlying business assumptions, that kind of change takes longer and hopefully lasts longer.

We're in a situation where turnarounds and quick fixes aren't enough. There's a sober mood everywhere. China is still booming, but its boom creates problems for others in Asia. No one I know is exuberant. The assumption in the 1990s was that you could declare yourself a capitalist country and everything else would take care of itself. Building institutions and creating trust and confidence take time.

I have enormous hopes for the benefits of the digital and Internet age. There have been tremendous improvements in education, and many businesses are more efficient internally. In education, technology can empower. There are already results available from the empowerment of teachers, and enormous potential is still available. In healthcare, physicians and providers can be empowered through having less paperwork and having the ability to get information faster and so on. If you can get the result of a medical test in minutes rather than hours, it can save lives.

The potential of technology remains very great, but we're in a period in which companies aren't spending money, and we're in the era's infancy. We lived through a period of peace and prosperity, and now we've had some crises and perhaps a challenge to some of the assumptions of Western capitalism. Now there's a cooling-off period. But new technology is fundamental and will make a difference.

So in the long run I am optimistic. I believe that if corporate citizenship and social entrepreneurship continue to flourish, we'll find new solutions and take them to new countries. Business has a pivotal role to play because business disciplines are very beneficial in creating any kind of change. And business enterprise creates the jobs that bring prosperity.

CHAPTER 7

Managing
Talent

William Shockley was a British-born research scientist who worked at the Bell Laboratories during the postwar period developing the transistor. In 1947 Shockley was recognized as the coinventor of the transistor, and in 1956 he was awarded a Nobel Prize for his efforts. In 1955, he left the Bell Labs to found his own company, Shockley Semiconductor Laboratory, in Palo Alto, Santa Clara County, California. His academic reputation attracted some of the finest minds in electronics to his company. Among them were Robert Noyce and Gordon Moore of Moore's law fame, who went on to cofound Intel; Julius Blank; Victor Grinich; Eugene Kleiner; Jean Hoerni; Jay Last; and Sheldon Roberts.

Unfortunately, Shockley's management skills fell far short of his academic prowess. To him people were dispensable. When he was asked whether his wife liked California, he replied: "She didn't like it, so I had to get a new wife." This anecdote seems to sum up his approach to human resources.

Not surprisingly, staff morale at Shockley's lab soon deteriorated. Eventually, Eugene Kleiner wrote a letter to a friend of his father who worked at an investment bank. The gist of the letter was that there was a group of seven scientists at Shockley Semiconductors who wanted to move en masse to another company.

Arthur Rock, a Harvard MBA at the investment bank, read the letter. Rock suggested that the seven should leave to start their own company. Rock secured funding from the inventor and entrepreneur Sherman Fairchild. Adding Bob Noyce to their number, the group started Fairchild Semiconductor in 1957.

Fairchild Semiconductor went on to revolutionize the world of computing through its work on the silicon transistor. As important, it threw off a slew of talented individuals who went on to start up some of the best-known companies in Silicon Valley.

Intel (Bob Noyce and Gordon Moore), Advanced Micro Devices (Jerry Sanders), and National Semiconductor (Charlie Sporck) were all spin-offs from Fairchild.

The defection of the so-called traitorous eight also played a major role in spawning the professional venture capital industry as a by-product. Arthur Rock and Eugene Kleiner became two of Silicon Valley's most respected VCs. Shockley's misguided approach to human resources inadvertently laid the cornerstone of Silicon Valley.

Talent-spotting companies have always fought with one another to attract the most able executives. At the end of the 1990s McKinsey & Company suggested that this perennial issue was set to become much more important. A McKinsey consultant, Steven Hankin, coined the phrase the *war for talent* to describe what it anticipated happening and what largely did happen.

McKinsey argued that there wouldn't be enough senior management talent to go around and that companies would have to find new and better ways to attract and retain high-caliber managers.

The 1997 research, based on a study of 77 large U.S. companies and carried out by five McKinsey consultants across North America, indicated that the battle for talent was already fierce. "Many American companies are already suffering a shortage of executive talent," said the report's authors. "Three-quarters of corporate officers surveyed said their companies had 'insufficient talent sometimes' or were 'chronically talent-short across the board.'"[1]

One of the most interesting aspects of the McKinsey research was that it attempted to define what it actually meant by the term *managerial talent*. This definition retains an element of vagueness but gives a real sense of the general nature of modern management: "Managerial talent is some combination of sharp strategic mind, leadership ability, emotional maturity, communication skills, the ability to attract and inspire talented people, entrepreneurial instincts, functional skills, and the ability to deliver results."[2]

The war for talent highlighted three trends. First and in many ways most serious was that in the United States at least, demand for executives appears to be moving in the opposite direction to supply. Until the late 1990s, the executive population had risen roughly in line with gross domestic product

(GDP). Demographers anticipated that the number of 35- to 44-year-olds in the workforce would fall.

At the same time the pace of change in the business world made it increasingly difficult for companies to predict the management capacity and skills mix they would require five years down the road.

The second factor in the escalating talent war was the fact that the demands companies place on executives were—and still are—increasing. Today, an increasingly complex global market requires more sophisticated management skills, including international experience, cultural fluency, technological literacy, and entrepreneurial flair.

The third factor was the rise of many high-potential small and medium-size companies; this meant that large companies had to compete with—and provide career opportunities, excitement, and earnings on a par with—their smaller brethren.

At the time, the solution, said the McKinsey consultants, lay in elevating talent management to a burning corporate priority. This means creating and refining an employee value proposition—senior management's answer to why a talented employee should work for the company rather than a competitor—and, critically, continuing to develop a company's people.

The Hard Side of the Soft Stuff

The war for talent pushed the role of managing human resources up the executive agenda. Historically, the world of human resources (HR) was regarded as peripheral, apart from the discipline of hard, analytical rigor. Among those most compellingly challenging this assumption is Dave Ulrich, who has spent his career pushing HR into the managerial mainstream.

Ulrich, a professor of business at the Ross School of Business at the University of Michigan and cofounder of the RBL Group, has written more than 15 books on HR and leadership.

What first ignited your interest in HR?
Well, a long time ago I was interested in how you build organizations that succeed and how you do that in a sustainable way. So I put in some time studying issues around change and how you make change happen, and what I discovered is that a lot of the change work didn't have sustainability. And the sustainability comes from the infrastructure of the firm; it's the staffing, training, compensation, communications. And so my take on HR was, How do you meld three circles? One is business strategy: Where are we going. The second is change: How do you make things happen? The third is HR: How do you sustain them? And I've tried to work, I think, at the intersection of those three circles throughout my career.

Your book HR Transformation *called for a change in the way HR is organized. Why?*
When I do seminars, one of the questions I often ask is, What's the biggest challenge you face in your job today? And when I'm working with HR people, a big percentage of the time, they say they're really worried about this compensation concern, a staffing issue, a

retention issue, a training issue, or building their personal credibility. What I like to suggest is that what we need to look at is the outcome or what we deliver.

So when we think about HR transformation, we like to not start with, How do you change the structure? How do you change the HR system? Instead, we like to start with, What's the outcome, and what's the business context in which that outcome occurs?

The tool that we've given people is a really simple one. We say, What's the biggest challenge you face in your job today: a staffing concern, a pay concern? Then we suggest use two words: *so that*—so that my organization moves more quickly to markets, so that in an economic recession I can build market share. When we ask at least two *so that*s, we go from the activity to the outcome for the business context.

Where I like to start the HR discussion is around the business context.

Is there a sense that HR can be an internally focused activity?

Quite often. When we say to an HR group, "Who are the customers you serve?" a preponderance of the time people will say, "We're here to serve the employees." We come back and say, "True, but incomplete." The customers of an HR group are the customers of a company: people who take money out of their purse or their wallet and give it to the company. And if HR people have that mindset, we then don't want to be the employer of choice in the HR line; we want to be the employer our customers would choose. We don't want to build on your strengths, which is another popular line in our field; we want to build on strengths that will strengthen others. That shifts HR from delivering value inside the company to delivering value outside.

HR often feels like a marginal activity in some corporations.

In some corporations it probably should be, because the HR work is focused on administrative transactions, which have to be done and have to be done well. But when an executive says, "Our people are our most important asset," I like to say to that executive, "You now have another phrase: Our people are really our customers' most important asset." Are we building people talent inside the company that will create value for the customers outside?

For example, if we're running a training program, if your customer sat through this training program or observed what you were teaching or was the recipient of what you taught, would that customer buy more products or services from you?

A lot of companies have done values statements, which is a wonderful thing to do, but the real value of values is if you took that value statement to your best customers and showed it to them and said, "Are these the values you want us to be good at?" To really begin to link the internal work with the external, and then to the customers say, "What do we now have to do to make these values real to you?" And then say to them, "When we do that, will you buy more from us?" The line of sight between the inside HR work and the outside customer expectations is where the ultimate value will be sustained.

But do people with an HR background actually get to the top of organizations?
It's often people in finance and marketing, but I'm not sure that that's necessarily a criterion. It says that the only way you're a good financial person is if you become CEO. Implicitly it says that the only way you're a good HR person is if you leave the function. What I would hope we'd have is HR people who really are business-literate. We call it being a business ally, but it's having economic and business literacy so that when we sit and engage in a discussion with the business leader, we can talk about business terms, we can talk about CAGR [compound annual growth rate] and return on net present value, we can talk about the business terms that will help the business be successful.

It's easy for it to be great HR when you're successful. When you're less successful, HR becomes more marginalized.
Actually, it's interesting. In down markets, when we're struggling, in some ways the talent organization issues become even more critical, because you're under a

greater magnifying glass. Sometimes in up markets, the rising tide covers ineffective systems.

In a recession what we've seen in employee engagement surveys is what may be a false positive. A lot of companies are having very high employee engagement survey scores. It's kind of a gratitude effect. I have a job, and we've let go all the people who weren't happy, and I'm grateful to have a job.

The reason HR really matters more than ever is that if in this downturn you've got employees who have a gratitude effect—I'm happy that I have a job, I'm engaged—what's going to happen when the recession ends and the economy turns back up is that firms that didn't treat their people well through good human resource practices will probably have a slough-off in their engagement and talent indexes.

Memories are longer than recessions. On the other hand, firms that treated their people well will continue to have that increase [in employee engagement]. So I think in a downturn, while it's seductive to say, Well, we don't have to do HR work, because memories are longer than recessions, we actually have to do it very, very aggressively. In up markets, when the markets are good, employees have a choice. They can move elsewhere, so we also have to build good human resources systems to maintain and keep our people.

The HR field has gone through two phases in the talent field and is now moving to a third. One is competence: Do employees have the skills to do the job? Do they have the brainpower to do it? Second is engagement: Do we have their hands and their feet? And I think often we have hands and feet. People show up. Employees may be there, but they may not be fully engaged; they may not be fully participating. We've been doing quite a bit of work lately around the issue of how you build an organization that captures not just your brains, your hands, and your feet but your heart and your soul. When you want to create an organization that captures that, we've called that building abundance and a sense of meaning. The employee value proposition of the future will not just be around terms and conditions at work but will be about meaning and abundance at work. When you can shape that in the organization, we think then not just the engagement scores go up with your hands and your feet, but your heart and your soul go up too. And that's the direction in which the employee and talent proposition will head.

So it's the HR department's job to create meaning in the organization?

It's the HR department's job to be the architect of meaning. I think line managers are the owners. When we build a house with an architect, the architect gives us a blueprint, gives us a framework, gives us models, gives us ideas. Ultimately, as the owner of the house, we make the final decision. I think line managers are ultimately accountable and responsible for that sense of meaning among employees.

In HR Transformation you talk about four phases. The first phase is business context, the second phase is the outcomes, the third phase is HR redesign, and the fourth phase is HR accountability. Could you explain how those phases work?

Sure. Let's assume that for whatever reason a chief HR officer wants to transform his or her HR department. I think you begin by answering the question, Why?

Let's assume that you're doing a presentation to an executive committee and seeking approval. The first few slides would be, here is the business context that is driving the rationale for transformation. Here is why we are doing it: markets are changing, shareholder value is falling on the intangible side, we're getting less customer revenue from targeted customers, employee productivity retention. So we've got the why; we've got the rationale.

The second set of slides, which is phase 2, is, What is it we're going to deliver? What's the outcome if we do this transformation well? The outcome is not an activity but a set of capabilities. A capability represents what the organization is good at doing. Are we good at moving quickly to markets, are we good at innovation, are we good at customer service, are we good at managing cost?

HR's transformation starts with specifying why we're doing it; it then moves to what it is that we'll get when we do it. Phase 3 is how we go about it. Number one, how do we change the HR function—our strategy, our structure? How do we build the function? HR is systems help; our delivery system helps.

Number two, how do we align, integrate, and innovate our HR practices, our people, performance, communication, organizational practices?

Number three, how do we upgrade our HR professionals? What skills and knowledge do they need to be successful?

And then phase 4: Who is accountable for this work, what's the role of the HR person, what's the role of the line manager, what's the role of the employee, what's the role of the outside advisor? Those four phases give us, if you will, a blueprint or a road map for how to go about doing HR transformation.

Ready for Talent

Since the 1997 McKinsey report, companies have looked long and hard at how best to attract, retain, and motivate talented individuals. The stakes have become ever higher. Managing talent is no longer simply about keeping career execs happy. Increasingly, companies—sometimes entire industries—are hostage to the brilliance (or otherwise) of a small number of individuals. The computer gaming industry is an example of this in which a small number of game designers hold enormous power.

This theme was powerfully explored by Rob Goffee and Gareth Jones of IE Business School in their *Harvard Business Review* article "Leading Clever People" and their book *Clever*.[3] "Talking to leaders and followers, it was clear that expectations had changed. Followers did not expect to be told what to do. They wanted leadership with respect as well as rewards. Similarly, leaders realized that certain of their followers generated huge amounts of value for the organization. Their most valuable people were crucial to the success of the organization and yet, at the same time, often the most difficult to lead," Goffee and Jones told us.

Goffee and Jones's checklist for leading clever people advises that leaders must acknowledge the diversity of the knowledge of the clever people they employ, exhibit competence to them, win resources and give them space, act as an umbrella to protect them from troublesome organizational politics, encourage failure, recruit clever people, give direction as motivation is usually not an issue, be accessible, encourage recognition from outside, and create a simplified rule environment.

"The challenge facing the leaders of today and of the foreseeable future is how to build organizations that can convert this potential value into actual value in the highly competitive world of the knowledge economy," say Goffee and Jones. "That is a substantial challenge, and it is one that requires a new style of leadership. In the world we are describing, leaders can no longer be the sole driving force for progress. They are not the ones who lead the charge up the mountain. Rather, they must identify the clever people with the potential to reach the summit, connect them with others, and help them get there. Once leadership was all about planting your flag on the summit and standing heroically for a photograph. Now the leader is the one pacing anxiously at base camp waiting to hear good news."

Among those offering other useful insights into managing talent is Doug Ready, founder and president of the International Consortium for Executive Development Research (ICEDR).

Ready has studied the dynamics of talent management from a variety of angles.

What first ignited your interest in this area?
It's been a journey. Let me start with some of the earlier work that I did, which was all about building an enterprise leadership capability. I wrote a *Sloan Management Review* article called "Leading at the Enterprise Level" that was really about the transition from being a unit leader, whether it's the unit of analysis of the business function or geography, to become an enterprise leader. And in doing that work I realized that's one of the toughest transformations that a leader has to make, and that got me investigating the world of talent management.

How can organizations do a better job of spotting talent earlier in people's careers? How can they provide the developmental opportunities for them to be able to progress instead of growing up in silos that get hardened and then make it much more difficult for leaders in organizations to not only move across those silos but also collaborate? And that's a critical capability for the future. So the work in enterprise leadership migrated into realizing that to build great companies we had to have companies that were committed to talent management and leadership development.

It's universally acknowledged that people are an organization's greatest assets. So why do organizations find it so difficult to develop their talent?

Part of the reason is that these organizations are driven to perform, and so it's a lot easier and a lot safer for them to go with the talent that's ready now as opposed to investing in the development of people. So we have that pathology going on, plus we tend to hire and promote people who look and think the same way we look and think.

With globalization and diversity it becomes a big challenge for companies to begin to see what it is they really need in order to flourish. They have tended to be very conservative in terms of how they think about the world of talent management, not looking in nontraditional places for what that next generation of leader might look like and where they might be.

Your previous research looked at collective ambition and purpose.

That work largely came as a result of the global financial crisis. I was getting many calls from companies and organizations that were seeking help to guide them through a period that was not just a transformation but in this case a sea change, and they had not seen this level of disruption before. So the idea was to ask, Are there organizations out there that actually are able to not only get through this crisis but thrive through it?

That set me on this course to begin to look at organizations to see how they were using this crisis as a platform for them to both transform and then, in some cases, to recommit to the things that made them great companies to begin with.

That's where we got into this concept of the glue and the grease. The glue is the cultural elements that really serve as the heritage of these organizations to begin with. But sticking with the glue will only get you stuck. At the same time organizations need to find enabling mechanisms that will make it easier for them to change, to adapt, and to be agile. It is this concept of leading with a sense of purpose, getting clear about the organization's vision, and making sure that strategic and operational initiatives were actually tied to that sense of purpose and vision that is the grease.

The glue was to look at this idea of saying, What is our brand promise? What are we all about, and what experiences are we providing and promising to our stakeholders? And are we really living up to that promise? It's this idea of marrying promises made with promises kept.

The idea of collective ambition is to enable companies to literally map out and chart a course or a compass, so to speak, to get them through the change journey, and it's been very powerful. Organizations such as the Four Seasons, such as Standard Chartered, that have had to navigate rather significant sea change–type transformations really picked up on the notion of collective ambition, and it helped their chief executives guide their organizations through this change.

What does a game-changing talent strategy look like? What are its hallmarks?

Many organizations are very adept at being value creators, but we're looking for the game changers. And the fundamental theory is that a game-changing company has got to be underpinned by having game-changing talent strategies.

We're looking at organizations that have mastered what we call a series of paradoxes. You think about the world and how it's growing, and virtually every company on the planet is looking to grow in Asia, and so they need talent management strategies that are globally scaled yet resonate on the ground locally. They need to have a strategic, capability-building orientation, yet at the same time they have to be operationally effective.

What I learned with the collective ambition work was that people are looking for a sense of connectedness, that talent strategies can help organizations build a sense of collective purpose, yet at the same time, a talent strategy has to work at the unit of Me Incorporated. So can I build a career here while I'm contributing to a collaborative, collective organization?

The last paradox is about committing to talent as an enduring mechanism yet at the same time not believing your own press releases and being regenerative and agile. It's the game-changing talent strategies that I think are the ones that are able to not only manage but master those four series of paradoxes very well.

*Are attitudes toward talent management and leader-
ship development different as you travel around the
world, or is there something universal here?*

The nature of the challenge is different. In Asia, for
example, you have a huge acquisition and retention
challenge, whereas in the more mature companies
you have an engagement challenge and a development challenge.

If you think about a talent management value
chain and how you manage the different points along
the continuum, depending on the growth cycle,
depending on the age and maturation of the organization, what its big challenges are, there are different
elements of that value chain that really jump out at
you as being most important.

CHAPTER 8

Managing Globally

Managing globally used to be the exception. Now most managers have an international dimension to their work even if they never leave their offices.

This evolution was explained to us by Erin Meyer, a professor at INSEAD and an expert on cross-cultural management. "Until probably seven or eight years ago mostly what people working across cultures needed to understand was how another culture was operating. It was usually about two cultures working together. So maybe you would have a French person who was wanting to better understand American management or an American who was wanting to understand the various management styles of different European countries.

"Today the landscape has changed entirely. A huge percentage of managers in multinational companies are in situations where they have team members from many different countries who are collaborating together and they have to understand not how do I manage one culture and how do they perceive me, but how do these various cultures on my team perceive one another and how can I improve the collaboration between those two cultures?"

Meyer, an American living in Paris, advocates cultural relativity as a useful means of understanding the new dynamics. This is how she explained it to us:

> You can't start thinking about global teamwork or multicultural interaction unless you think about relativity. Let me you give you an example. I was working with a global team a few months ago, and I had on this team a group of British people, a group of French people, and a group of Indians.
>
> At the beginning we had just French and British team members. I was talking to the British group and asked them, What's it like to work with the French? One of the British said, Well Erin, you know the French. They are very chaotic, they're disorganized, they're often late, they're always changing the topic in the middle of the meetings, so it's very difficult to follow them.
>
> A little later the Indian group joined, and I asked the Indians, What's it like to work with the French? They said, You know the French. They're so rigid, they're so unadaptable, they're so focused on the structure and timeliness of things that if you don't tell them

weeks in advance exactly what's going to happen in the meeting or in what order, it makes them very nervous.

So these two cultures have these totally opposite impressions of the same culture. That's cultural relativity. One of the things that managers need to understand is that just because your culture has one perception of a culture that you're working with, it doesn't mean another culture will have the same perception, and the goal that I have in my work is to present a framework that helps people decode the way these different cultures perceive one another. So it moves us from a cross-cultural space to a multicultural space.

Global Dilemmas

Probably the most influential thinker in the cross-cultural field is the Dutchman Fons Trompenaars, the author of one of the seminal books on the subject, *Riding the Waves of Culture*. We spoke with the voluble and engaging Trompenaars about the evolution of his work.

Why was there thirst for the subject at the time Riding the Waves of Culture *was published?*

It was the first time that a book was published that made the translation to What does it mean for management? There are other models or alternative models, but it's really the translation into what it means for a manager: What can I do with it?

The world has changed from, let's say, multilocality: you prepare yourself for Singapore, you prepare yourself for America. Now you hardly see that. People go to America but on the way have to deal with Mexicans, Canadians, Argentineans, and Venezuelans. So it's much more about leadership across cultures rather than preparing for a nation.

You talk about various dilemmas.
Once you recognize cultural differences—and a lot of work is about recognition—if you respect those differences, they turn into dilemmas. The real issue for people in business is, Okay, I know there are differences, I respect them. What do I do? That means you need to manage dilemmas.

Are cultures as different as they used to be?
Yes and no. Standardization, homogenization, also invites more difference. It's interesting: the more we homogenize, the more we want to be different. I've very often used a pendulum as a way of reflecting that. The more it swings at the bottom, the more it needs a nail to hold it together. However, if you make the nail as big as the pendulum, people start to get desperate; they want the swing. People are different.

It also shows in our databases, in the research we've done, that at some levels we homogenize in order to allow for differences at other levels.

Can you give an example?
The pizza is the most obvious one. You homogenize the base on which you add different toppings. Take

that as a metaphor. You have global organizations, and there are still some who want to have one culture worldwide and everything is detailed and codified into every aspect of how to do it. Then you have the multi-local organization where there are different activities and different operational modes across cultures.

And that's where we're going to with transcultural organizations. The transcultural organization knows exactly what to share to allow for more differences. For example, you might say we as a company want to reward high performance. The way high performance is defined and how we reward we leave it up to the country, but it's all based on high performance. It's also true with values. There are certain values, such as integrity, where we say we believe in integrity, but integrity is seen differently in America than in parts of Europe or in Asia.

So the idea, again, is that successful organizations know what to share and what to homogenize.

One of the things that were so influential was the four models of corporate cultures.

It's based on two major axes: the hierarchical and egalitarian type of relationships on one axis and on the other axis formal and more informal person-oriented relationships. If you combine those two axes, you get four types.

The Anglo-Saxon model combines an egalitarian ideology with class orientation. It is the *guided missile*, based on strategy, management by objectives, pay for performance. That model is contradicted by the hierarchical and person-oriented *family* culture. This is based on who you know rather than what you know. It is, if you like, management by subjectives. What motivates people here is the accumulation of power.

Then we have the combination of hierarchic with a more task and functional orientation: the *Eiffel Tower*. It's based on structure, management by job description. And what motivates people in the Eiffel Tower is the accumulation of expertise; that's why in Germany the symbol of that expertise is having a title.

Then we have the *incubator*, which is egalitarian and person-oriented: Silicon Valley, parts of Scandinavia. You manage by passion. They call their salary the monthly insult because the motivational principle is learning.

We have also seen that in innovative companies you go through the stages. You start with the incubator, two people with a great idea like Sergey Brin and Larry Page, but it grows and it gets into a leadership crisis. Then you need the family culture because the family includes the incubator.

The family grows and then gets into a crisis of its own, so you need the guided missile. It grows, and it gets into the crisis of control. It needs the Eiffel Tower for execution and stability. Then finally it goes back into the incubator.

What we have found is that to be innovative you now need to take a fifth step that's called *exnovation*.

You have to go outside the company in order to be innovative. You need to combine business models and try to combine partners outside your industry.

You talk a lot about reconciling dilemmas; it underpins all of your work. What sorts of dilemmas are you thinking about? Are those dilemmas changing, and what do organizations need to do to tackle them?
We believe that the next fashion is coming. We had the fashion for efficiency and effectiveness; that all started in management at the beginning of the last century. Then we had the next fashion. Everything was about motivating people, and it killed itself, like the first fashion, by exaggeration.

Then we had the focus on clients, marketing, and sales; it, too, was killed by exaggeration. The next exaggeration was shareholder value. I remember I wrote an article with the title "Shareholder Value, the Value Created That People Never Share," and I predicted it would kill itself.

The next fashion is corporate social responsibility. But every value of any stakeholder is only one way of looking at things, and if you do it at the cost of other values, it's not sustainable.

The issue is the dilemmas created between the stakeholders. So we have now identified 18,000 dilemmas and selected a top 10. I will give you some examples:

Developing people versus cost consciousness. If you go for cost, you don't develop your people. If you develop the people, you can't be cost-conscious. How do you reconcile that?

Equal opportunities versus positive discrimination. If you go for one or the other, it's not sustainable. You need to combine them.

Serving what your customer wants versus following what society tells you. If you are PepsiCo and you are into snacks and sugared water because the customer wants it, it's not sustainable. Lawmakers say we have to be careful about our health, so it's not sustainable for PepsiCo. You need to combine the two.

Global versus local. These types of dilemmas between stakeholders are the ones that we encounter most, and we help clients on three levels. What are your dilemmas? How confident are you that your leaders can deal with those dilemmas? How does the corporate goal give you a context in which you can serve those dilemmas?

A Cultural Tour

Theory is useful, but on the ground what are the core skills required of the global executive? Andrew Kakabadse of the United Kingdom's Henley Business School has worked around the globe in a variety of capacities over the last three decades. His top-team database of corporate executives covers 17 nations and many thousands of private and public sector organizations. The study of the strategic skills of top teams has now extended into Japan, China, Hong Kong, and the United States. Kakabadse's books include the idiosyncratically-titled *Rice Wine with the*

Minister: Distilled Wisdom to Manage, Lead, and Succeed on the Global Stage.

Tell us something about the title of your book.
The title evolved from a trip to China. I was in one of the central provinces, and a minister asked me to talk about the future of China and the importance of developing managers. Over lunch, I was offered a small glass of the special rice wine of the region. Turned out that it was a polite and friendly trap: I was asked to toast each person at the table, which meant I had to drink 21 glasses of the wine. Everyone else had to drink only one or two. Somehow I managed to survive the social test without passing out. They wanted to see how—make that if—I could handle the challenge. It ultimately made me, for the moment, one of the group.

Is one of your points that business travelers need to be able to navigate situations like that?
Yes. If you plan to do business in cultures around the world, you have to be able to navigate many social challenges. You have to be able to find out very quickly what the key dos and don'ts are in each area. When I counsel executives who are planning a trip to a country they have never visited before, I always ask them many questions:

What have you read about the place you're going to? Who is your guide? Who is your home country's ambassador there? How important is it to have good relationships with your business counterparts? Do you know how to talk to people openly? (It varies from place to place.) If you're going to upset somebody, do you know how to do that well as well?

But busy executives can't become experts on every country they might visit, can they?

That's exactly right. You cannot become an expert on all cultures, but you can become an expert on how to get into a culture.

You talk about reach, readiness, and rollout. Can you explain?

First, you must be willing to reach out to a new culture whose history, traditions, and cultural norms may be vastly different from your own. This means first and foremost that you have to be able and willing to learn.

It's important to find out what's happening in the country right now, what's happening in the communities you plan to visit. But it's also important to prepare yourself by reviewing some of the country's history, hopefully drawing some connections between what happened in the past and what's going on in today's business world.

In many ways, reaching out in another country is not unlike reaching out among your own top executive team. It is likely that you won't be successful bonding with someone from another country if you haven't bonded well with your own management team. From my experience, many top team members don't have the same vision and values, and it's often because those team members are ensconced in their own corporate world.

Now stretch to a larger canvas: the world. You have to be able to embrace, enjoy, and elevate diversity by learning how to integrate the complexities of another culture with your own heritage. If you can't reach out intellectually, if you can't reach out personally, you can't put your executive team together and you quite probably can't reach out and win the confidence of those in another country. In the end, when I talk about reach, I'm talking about cultivating the ability to reach out and win the trust of people you work with no matter where they may come from on the planet.

Then it's important to augment reach with being ready? One of the big concerns with readiness, funnily enough, is partly the person who aspires to be a global business leader. Here again I ask prospective executives a lot of questions: Are you ready in terms of resilience? Can you handle strain and pressure? Can you fly many times around the globe many times a year? Are you fit physically? The point here is that doing business around the world is a skill that has to be developed on a personal level.

There's a second level of readiness: Is your organization ready to engage in global business? You have to be able to structure your company in such a way that its organizational chart and its resources can maximize the chances of success in working with companies rooted in another culture. Those you will be meeting as you move closer to a contract to work together will need to understand whom they should contact when the inevitable problems arise. After all, successful relations between top executives are most likely the start of new relationships up and down two organizations. So you have to be ready to explore and explain whether your director of quality does the same kind of things that their director with the same title does.

Third, you mention the importance of rollout.
When you have reached the point at which you personally can reach out and you, as a person and as an organization, are ready to engage business worldwide, it's time to move, to roll out everything you've got. The starting block for doing business globally is the point at which you are ready to set up a first meeting with someone in another country whom you do not know. You have to know how to move on that desire. That means you will have to have a firm grasp of your business network (who knows someone whom you'd like to meet?), your customer targets (which companies will most likely want to do business with yours?), and your product positioning (what makes a product appealing in San Francisco, and how is it different in New Delhi?).

There are many managers today who take pride in being able to say, "I can ring up Nelson Mandela as well as ring up this sales agent in China." But their ability to roll out an overture to either person took much time and work in the past. And this is precisely why I stressed reach and readiness before rollout: you can never be sure what political ramifications might emerge from what you thought was a "simple" business transaction. For example, if you're going to try to acquire a company in Indonesia, it's certain to have political repercussions. All of the stakeholders tied to your target acquisition will have to be accounted for, tended to, and satisfied. It's unwise to roll out until you know your company can succeed.

Can you give an example of how your three goals actually played out in a real case?

I worked with a company that tried to sell its wares in Japan and, unfortunately, tried to sell them in much the same way it did in Europe. Poor reach, not ready, unsuccessful rollout. While trying to make the sale, the company discovered that the Japanese kitchen was much smaller than one in Europe. This turned out to be a setback that could have been foreseen. For example, Japanese housewives could not handle one of their products (and it was a rice cooker!). Europeans liked their rice cooker to be on all day and wanted to use it for multiple purposes. By contrast, the rice cooker in Japan is to be used for only one purpose at one time. In time, my organization was able to help them with issues like this.

How about a company that did things right?

Another company I know wanted to sell pharmaceutical products in Africa. The company's managers took special note to identify the possible race issues in different parts of that continent. It also had to note the differences between selling in urban versus selling in rural areas. And it had to make sure it had the pricing right so the company was not viewed as being mercenary. In essence, pricing was a political issue, and the company was very smart in how it handled this matter. It used pricing to prove that the company's responsibility as a corporation was to help people at the grass roots, people with limited financial resources. Moreover, the company sent employees to various villages where not only had they positioned their products to deal with AIDS but they also made an effort to improve the supply of water and electricity. Why do all this? The company was not only showing a sense of social responsibility; it also improved the whole community to make it a much more sophisticated market—with the opportunity for expanded business contracts in the future much more likely. That was a fantastic example of thinking broadly.

What are the characteristics you feel are essential to anyone who aspires to be a global business leader?

First, he or she must demonstrate a commitment to learning, which to my mind goes far beyond simple curiosity. Learning is an intellectual process; your head has to work to look out for new facts, new concepts, new ideas. It's not enough to pack your mind with product and marketing knowledge and then shut down your brain. You must have a mindset that looks out for and absorbs new knowledge.

Second, I would cite personal resilience. You do have to be personally tough. You may give the appearance of being soft and charming, but inside you need to be tough. When you travel the world on business, you will eat exotic foods at odd times, meet loads of people—20 in a day, 30 in a weekend—and sleep less (and perhaps poorly). You will have to be resilient to make sure your stomach can adapt to provide your body energy. You will have to enable your mind to bounce back, to work overtime, so that the thirtieth person you talk to feels that you are listening as intently as if the meeting were your first engagement of the trip. When you can't listen well (or if you haven't disciplined yourself to listen), it shows, and actually that's an insult. It's very insulting for a senior manager talking to someone from another country to appear not to be interested in the new acquaintance. And you will have to have enough stamina that short sleep is sufficiently restful to allow you to operate competently and think clearly.

Last but perhaps most important, you must know how to handle personal relationships. Humility goes a long way. Making sure that you invite people to talk to you about their problems and concerns goes a long way. It also provides you with valuable information for the future. In sum, the more people trust you, the more they will feel that they can speak openly and thus the more you have an opening to form a lasting business relationship. And that is an asset that is far more valuable than a bottle of even the best rice wine.

CHAPTER 9

Managing
Emotionally

Over the last century as management theory and practice have evolved, emotions have largely been ignored. Managers
generally were assumed to be unemotional men in suits, and
many were. Now, however, the full range of human emotions is
on display in any organization. All life is there.

But how can—and should—managers make sense of this
emotional potpourri? Three thinkers offer different ways forward. First, Howard Gardner offers insight into the qualities
of thinking that will allow people to survive and prosper in the
twenty-first century both in work and in life generally. Second,
Daniel Goleman provides the theory of emotional intelligence,
neat but far-ranging. Third, Dan Pink offers insights into the
emotional activity of selling, essential to any manager.

Renowned worldwide for his theory of multiple intelligences, Howard Gardner is the John H. and Elisabeth A. Hobbs Professor of Cognition and Education at the Harvard Graduate School of Education and adjunct professor of psychology at Harvard University.

Moving on from his multiple intelligence work, Gardner is now focusing on the future and "the cognitive abilities that will command a premium in the years ahead." He argues that "five minds" will be vital to future success.

You say these five ways of thinking will be even more important in the future. What's changed?

There are three significant trends in the modern world which establish the background for these kinds of minds.

Number one: the importance of technology, particularly computers. Computers can do almost everything that human beings can, so the things we are going to value human beings for will be very different.

The second thing is globalization. It is about understanding the interconnectivity of the world and the kinds of things that you need in order to be able to function in a world that was not nearly so interconnected 50 years ago.

And the third big change?

The third change has to do with diversity. We evolved as a species having contact with about 150 people, most of whom looked like us and were probably related to us.

Today diversity stares you in the face in a way that was inconceivable when I was growing up. I hardly need to say this in a place like London, where you have millions of people, many from non-English backgrounds and many with different religious and cultural backgrounds.

So there is a sense that we can be in contact with, and have influence on, everybody around the world and vice versa.

And the five minds in the book are the ways of thinking that are best suited to this new world you are describing. What are the five minds?
Well, the first three are the kinds of things that I have been talking about for a very long time: the disciplined mind, the synthesizing mind, and the creating mind.

The last two, though, have more to do with the human sphere: the respectful mind and the ethical mind. Over the last decade a lot of my research has focused on these two.

Could you explain a little more about each mind?
The disciplined mind is knowing something very well, being an expert in an art or craft or profession and keeping it up. That means being disciplined. If you don't have a disciplined mind, you really don't have a job at all, or you end up working for somebody who does.

The synthesizing mind stems from the fact that we all are deluged with information. How do you decide what to pay attention to, what to ignore, how to put it together in a way that makes sense to you? How do you communicate your synthesis to other people? That's probably the most distinctive mind, because I've given a label to something that people haven't really talked about much before.

And the creative mind?

The third kind of mind, the creating mind, is basically coming up with something new that eventually affects how other people are and think. If it is "thinking outside the box," then the disciplined and synthesizing minds provide the box, and for many people, that's enough and you wouldn't want everybody to be creative or the world would be too chaotic.

But for some cutting-edge or eccentric few, it's thinking and doing stuff that really ends up affecting a lot of other people.

And what of the remaining two minds, which your recent work has focused on more closely?

The respectful mind is very simple and certainly goes back to prebiblical, preliterate times. Basically it means giving other people the benefit of the doubt, trying to know them, trying to understand them, not being too judgmental, and being capable of forgiveness.

It begins at birth. Infants notice how other people treat one another and how they treat themselves. The reason it's so acutely important nowadays is because of the diverse society we live in. My belief in the importance of the respectful mind has caused me to change my views about issues such as whether women students in France should be allowed to wear the hijab.

Which leaves the ethical mind.

The last mind, the ethical mind, is one that I've been working on intensively for a decade-plus, and it's a little bit more technical to define.

The ethical mind is a mind that is capable of abstraction. And the ethical mind basically can think about oneself abstracting. So I'm not just Howard Gardner, but I'm Howard Gardner who is a journalist, an author, a lawyer, an engineer, whatever. I have a role occupationally, and I'm also a citizen; I'm a citizen of my community, my city, my state, my region, my nation, the world.

The ethical mind asks, What are my responsibilities as a journalist, what are my responsibilities as a citizen of London, the United Kingdom, the planet?

What relevance does the five minds concept have for organizations in the future, and does it apply more broadly than in business?

My work has an "is" aspect: What are the minds that will be at a premium in the future? It also has an "ought" aspect: What sorts of minds should be cultivated?

Individuals involved in management need to think about their own minds and the extent to which those minds embody discipline, synthesizing capacity, creativity, respect, and ethics. If they are lacking on these dimensions, what might they do to enhance them? How should they assemble teams, and can one person's strength compensate for the weaknesses of others?

Could you give some examples with reference to some of the individual minds and how they relate to a non-business organization such as the United Kingdom's National Health Service, for instance?

Respect and ethics are good examples. The NHS needs to understand and know how to deal with its diverse populations. Here both respect and ethics become vital. Unless there is an atmosphere of respect, individuals will not trust one another and relations will deteriorate.

Ethics entails an understanding of responsibilities attendant to a specific role. It is vital for members of the NHS to behave in an ethical way and to be able to assume that their peers will also behave ethically. And in those cases where ethical norms are clearly violated, the question of consequences looms large.

One cannot guarantee, of course, that patients will be respectful and/or ethical. But to the extent that the NHS embodies these virtues in its own interactions with patients, the chances are enhanced that the patients will reciprocate.

You also talk about the concept of good work.

I define good work as work that is technically excellent, personally engaging, and carried out in an ethical manner. When pressures are too great, any of the three Es can suffer.

So, for example, when physicians or nurses are asked to do too much, they become stressed and risk burnout; the factor of engagement is undermined. Excellence can also be at risk.

Threats to ethics come from the overall ambience of a community. When a community comes to value money, power, or success over all other priorities, individuals have little incentive to be honest, be responsible, or treat others with integrity.

And that also applies to nonbusiness organizations?

Yes, a public sector or voluntary organization should embrace a contrasting set of values having to do with pride in services well rendered and in top results. But the specter of monetary success is often very powerful, and unless it is counteracted by strong contrasting norms, it is likely to prevail.

What about the synthesizing mind?

Nowadays we are all inundated with information. The premium is to figure out what to pay attention to, what to ignore, how to organize it so that it makes sense to oneself, and then how to convey it so that it makes sense to others.

A fortunate few can figure out how to synthesize well, with little help from others. Most of us, however, need all the help we can get in synthesizing. I think this is a particularly acute need in highly innovative fields such as IT [information technology] and medical science where information compounds at a feverish pace and lives may be at stake.

In a future world in which the five minds are valued, nurtured, and prevalent, how do you see work changing?

I would love to live in a world characterized by good work: work that is excellent, engaging, and carried out ethically. In such a world, one could count on service being delivered reliably, with care, and with expertise.

Obviously, respect and ethics are essential for good work to be carried out. But only when practitioners have mastered their disciplines well, know how to synthesize, and can, when appropriate, come up with creative solutions to problems will this become a reality for most organizations.

Emotional Intelligence

Daniel Goleman is among the most influential thinkers to hit the business world in recent years. The bearded psychologist and former journalist has spread the gospel of emotional intelligence (EQ) to a largely grateful business world. It is based on the notion that the ability of managers to understand and manage their own emotions and relationships is the key to better business performance.

His 1997 book *Emotional Intelligence* has more than 5 million copies in print and was on the *New York Times* bestseller list for 18 months. His follow-up book *Working with Emotional Intelligence* applied his ideas to the business world. Next, *Primal Leadership* makes the case for cultivating emotionally intelligent leaders. In it, Goleman and coauthors Richard E. Boyatzis and Annie McKee explore how the four domains of emotional intelligence—self-awareness, self-management, social awareness, and relationship management—give rise to different styles of leadership. These constitute a leadership repertoire that enlightened leaders can master to maximize their effectiveness.

Goleman argues that human competencies such as self-awareness, self-discipline, and empathy are more important than qualities such as a high IQ both in life and in business. In demanding jobs in which an above-average IQ is a given, superior emotional capability gives leaders an edge. At senior levels, emotional rather than rational intelligence marks the true leader. This is supported by studies of outstanding performers that show that about two-thirds of the abilities that set star performers apart are based on emotional intelligence. Against this, only one-third of the skills that matter relate to raw intelligence (as measured by IQ) and technical expertise.

The good news is that emotional intelligence can be learned. There are five dimensions to this, he says, each of which is the foundation for specific capabilities of leadership:

1. **Self-awareness.** We seldom pay attention to what we feel. A stream of moods runs in parallel to our thoughts.

Our moods and previous emotional experiences provide a context for our decision making.

2. **Managing emotions.** All effective leaders learn to manage their emotions, especially the big three of anger, anxiety, and sadness. This, in the self-improvement argot, is a decisive life skill.

3. **Motivating others.** According to Goleman, the root meaning of *motive* is the same as the root of *emotion*: "to move."

4. **Showing empathy.** The flip side of self-awareness is the ability to read emotions in others.

5. **Staying connected.** Emotions are contagious. There is an unseen transaction that passes between us in every interaction that makes us feel either a little better or a little worse. Goleman calls this a "secret economy." He, however, has unearthed a far more open economy.

We began by asking about timing.

Emotional intelligence isn't a new phenomenon; it's always been there. So why has it become so important in today's business world?

It has always been a factor in success individually, particularly in business, but that fact hasn't been clearly identified until recently. Two things: there's been a convergence of forces that have called it to collective attention. One is the fact that in the last 10 years there's been a critical mass of research in science—brain science and behavioral science—that makes it clear that there is a capacity called emotional intelligence.

The notion itself was articulated first in 1990, so it's quite a new notion. Two Yale psychologists first came up with the term *emotional intelligence*, Peter Salovey and John Mayer. They wrote an article in what frankly was a very obscure psychology journal, but I was a journalist at the *New York Times* and my beat was brain and behavioral science, and one of the things I did was to scour the scientific literature looking for important new findings and concepts, and I thought that was an extremely important concept. I went on to write the book about it.

Meanwhile, companies had been doing internal studies quite independent of the notion of emotional intelligence, looking at what distinguished star performers in a given field, say, the head of a division or a sales team. The studies compared those star performers with people at the mean who were just average performers, trying to distinguish and distill the specific abilities that you found consistently in stars that you didn't see in others and then trying to hire people or promote people or develop people for those abilities. And when I wrote the book *Working with Emotional Intelligence* and then *Primal Leadership: Realizing the Power of Emotional Intelligence*, I was able to harvest hundreds of studies like that that had been done individually and independently for different organizations or looking at different roles within organizations, most of which were proprietary.

When I aggregated that data, what I found was that abilities like, for example, being able to manage your disturbing emotions, keeping them from dis-abling your ability to function; or empathy, being able to perceive how people are feeling and seeing things from their perspective; or the ability to cooperate well on a team, all of which are based on emotional intelligence, were the preponderance of the abilities that distinguished the best from the worst. And so there was this independent database which showed that emotional intelligence was extremely important in this context.

How do you score on your own EI measures? Are you emotionally intelligent?
Everyone has a profile of strengths and weaknesses. My own profile is, like anyone else's, rather uneven. But to get the most accurate, honest answer you'd have to ask the people who have worked with me—and my wife.

Is there a pattern? Do women tend to score higher, for example?
When you look at gender differences, you're look-ing at basically overlapping bell curves; there's more similarities than differences between the genders. But the differences that do emerge are that women tend to score better than men on average at empathy and some relationship abilities. Men tend to score bet-ter than women on emotional self-management and self-confidence. So I think each gender has its own strengths.

How much of EI is already determined before adult-hood?

The roots of each of these abilities start early in life. Every competence that distinguishes an outstanding leader in business has a developmental history, and if you ask people—and studies have been done—how did you become such a good team leader, for example, it will always start with a story, typically in middle school years at around age 11, 12, or 13. This is a real story. A woman who is a fantastic team leader was asked when this first started, and she said, "I moved to a new school and I didn't know anyone, so I thought I could meet people by joining the field hockey team. And it turned out I wasn't such a good player, but I was very good at teaching the new kids about the game. So I became a sort of de facto assistant coach." Then it turned out in her first job after university that she was in sales and no one showed her the ropes, so when she learned them, she spontaneously started teaching new people on the sales team. And she was so good at it that the company made a video about her, and that led to a fast track that resulted in her finally becoming senior vice president for sales. So each one of these abilities is learned over the course of life and is articulated, refined, and sharpened as you go up the ladder. That's an important point.

Are business leaders more emotionally intelligent today than in the past?

It's about as uneven as it ever was, frankly. One reason is that although there's clear data that these abilities matter, it doesn't mean that companies always use that to make decisions about who should be promoted. When it comes to who should be a leader, we are still prone to the Peter Principle: people being promoted to their level of incompetence. The most common error isn't that you're promoted because of the old boy network, which is the old story. The new story is that people tend to be promoted to leadership today because of technical expertise. You're a very good individual performer, and the automatic but mistaken assumption is made that of course you'll then be very good at leading a team of people like yourself. But the fallacy there is that what made you a good individual performer—your technical expertise—actually has nothing to do with what distinguishes people who are good team leaders. And the business world is rife with that. At the *New York Times* I saw it all the time. Journalists who were outstanding as journalists would become heads of desks or editors, which they were often terrible at.

What's the relationship between emotional intelligence and charisma? Presumably, charisma is partly in the eye of the beholder and partly has to do with certain skills that people project.

Charisma in terms of this model has to do with the ability to persuade and communicate. Bill Clinton is a beautiful example of someone who is fantastic at empathy and persuasion, which builds on empathy. If you meet Bill Clinton or are with him, you feel like you're the most important person in the world to him at that moment. He really tunes in. And he uses what he perceives to translate that into the language that will communicate most powerfully with you. Charismatic leaders do that with groups as a whole, and he certainly did. But you can also use him to illustrate that everyone has a profile of strengths and weaknesses in this domain. Because when it came to impulse control, he really flunked.

The other side of that is that as people become more emotionally competent, isn't there a danger that they become more Machiavellian?

Only in rare cases because Machiavellian behavior—which is where you take your self-interest over and above every other goal, so basically you'll do anything to get ahead—is a lapse in several emotional intelligence competencies, one of which is integrity. Another has to do with being able to cooperate well in a group. People who are Machiavellian, in other words who get a short-term gain, do it at a cost to other people. They leave a legacy of resentment, ill feeling, and anger, which very often catches up with them later in their careers.

One aspect of narcissistic people is that they often lack empathy, yet we still seem to want these people as leaders. Or perhaps we need it to get on.

I don't know that we do that any more. The most compelling data on that has to do with leadership style: the emotional climate the leader creates and how that translates into the motivation and ability of people to work at their best. The data looks like this: the people who are, for example, visionary, who can articulate a shared mission in a way that motivates and inspires people, create a very positive emotional climate, and so do leaders who are very good listeners and take a true interest in the individuals who work for them and try to understand what they want for their careers and how they can help them along. And so do leaders who know that having a good time together builds emotional capital for when the pressure is on. All those styles create the kind of climate where people can work at their best.

However, the leader who is the distant narcissist, the kind of command and control, do it because I say so leader, actually creates a very negative emotional climate. Especially if they become the kind of narcissistic leader who feels not only am I right, do it because I'm the boss, but who then blow up at people, get extremely impatient, hypercritical, and so on, which is a danger of that style. And that poisons the climate and alienates people. You lose talent, and people end up spending more time thinking about the boss and complaining about him or her than doing their work.

I'm not sure the data today supports the kind of mandate and power that we've given bosses like that in the past.

A particular area of interest to us is the genesis of big business ideas. Where did your ideas about EI come from?

The biggest influence on my thinking was my mentor at Harvard, the late David McClelland (1917–1998), who in the early 1970s, when I was a graduate student there working with him, wrote an article that at the time was a very radical proposal. He wrote it in the *American Psychologist.* If you want to hire the best person for a job, don't look at their academic grades, don't look at their test scores, don't look at their IQ, don't look at some personality profile, don't look at their connections or their social class, and certainly don't look at their letters of recommendation. He said that what you should first do is look at the people within your own organization who have held that post in the past and been outstanding at it and systematically compare them with the people who have held the post and done poorly or been average. And then determine what made the best so good and hire people with those capabilities. That is the basis for the methodology now called competence modeling, which was the data I harvested.

So he's had certainly the most direct influence both in showing me a method for having an informed answer to the question of what makes someone a truly good leader and also in making it possible 20 or 30 years later for me to harvest information from literally hundreds of organizations around the world.

What about Howard Gardner's work?

Howard Gardner, who was a grad student with me at Harvard in those days and a personal friend, also opened a door for me when he proposed the model of multiple intelligences, which says that in different domains there are different kinds of abilities that can be called an intelligence. Over and above the standard IQ model, which dates from the early twentieth century and around the 1900s, it's a narrow achievement model, just verbal and math abilities and a few spatial abilities. He argued that in every domain where there are competencies created and valued, there is a specific kind of intelligence. So, for example, there is a musical intelligence, and there's a kinesthetic intelligence in the domain of sports, ballet, and so on. He also said there are personal intelligences, and it's that domain of the personal intelligence that I've unpacked in explaining emotional intelligence.

Are IQ tests obsolete now?

No. IQ tests are very broad indicators of the fields that a person can qualify for, where a person can enter and hold a job. The problem with IQ tests is they don't take the next step. So let's say you're managing a pool of engineers in your corporation, or R&D scientists or accountants, lawyers, or whatever. IQ tests do not predict who among that pool of people now in the field itself will distinguish themselves over time as the most successful, the most effective, the most productive—whatever your measure of success is. It's interesting that even in the sciences IQ does not predict who over the course of a career will emerge as the most eminent scientist. Other abilities do, and they turn out to be the emotional intelligence abilities. So in other words, IQ is a threshold ability for a field, but it is not a distinguishing ability, and I'm most interested in the distinguishing abilities. IQ is a very good indicator, however, of what field you could enter.

How much do you think your journalistic skills have helped you?

I think they were invaluable because I was trained as a psychologist, and frankly, when I entered journalism, I was the slow kid on the block. My first job in journalism I had a very kindly managing editor, and after I'd write an article in typical journalese—I don't mean journalism; I mean typical academic journal style, which is Latinate, passive voice, absolutely flat prose—he would go through it literally line by line and word by word and show me how to change it to make it lively and engaging and make every word count and to eliminate 80 percent of the words I had chosen. He transformed my writing style. And I think my time at a daily newspaper at the *New York Times* just gave me more and more practice at a style that was engaging. Meanwhile, I was able to use my expertise in psychology to go into the academic literature and search for ideas that really did have impact and should have a wider audience. Those two things in combination gave me the abilities to write a book about emotional intelligence.

You say that emotional intelligence can be developed. What practical things can managers do to develop those abilities?

First of all, organizations can set up a format and make accessible a mode of learning that is appropriate to the emotional intelligence domain. What I mean by that is that you don't improve these abilities in the same way that you learn technical expertise like how to do a certain computer program, or in the mode that you learned when you went to school. It's a different part of the brain that's involved. And it doesn't learn as quickly as the neocortex. The model actually is skill acquisition. If there's something you're not as good at as you'd like to be, you can improve—that's the good news—but you need to do it in a way that brings along this part of the brain. First, you have to care. It has to be something you are motivated about. It has to be something that really matters to you because if you don't care, you won't make the necessary effort and it's going to take some months. Now, it doesn't take any extra time because you use your day-to-day encounters as the opportunities to practice and hone the improved mode.

So, for example, to take a common problem, you don't listen well. Someone walks into your office, and you start telling him what you think rather than first hearing what he has to say and making sure you understand it. Well, that's a choice point in which you can choose to make an effort to change, and instead of just jumping in and giving your opinion, you can make sure that you really have heard and understood. If you do that at every opportunity, what will happen is that slowly you're going to be building a new neural network; you are strengthening connections between brain cells so that your former default setting at the neural level, which was to jump in, now has an alternative path. You're strengthening the circuitry there. And there will come a day when you automatically sit back and listen to understand before you give your opinion; that means that the alternative circuit has become the new default option and is now the stronger pathway in the brain.

That kind of learning has been used successfully by my coauthor on *Primal Leadership*, a man called Richard Boyatzis at Case Western University School of Management. He's been doing it with his executive MBAs for 10 or 15 years. He's done follow-ups with them at the places where they work in which he asks other people to evaluate them on the behavior they tried to improve back in their MBA program. He's found that if you use this mode of learning, you can see the improvements seven years later; that's as long as he's done it. That's quite remarkable. Most business seminars or weekend seminars or even a week off site—if that's all you do, it won't be enough to make the requisite change. You really do need the sustained learning opportunity.

How does your message go down in India or China?
India is hugely taken with emotional intelligence. I must get several e-mails weekly from India from people who have read the book and want to apply it either in their graduate work or in the management of their companies.

China is a little different story. The last talk I gave in China was arranged by the government of Shanghai, talking to business leaders in the Shanghai community. Because of their entry into the WTO [World Trade Organization], Chinese leaders are realizing that they need to update their management abilities and skills to a world-class standard. So even though one of the things I'm talking about is shifting from a rather totalitarian control style, which was the pervasive style through China, to a more democratic style where leaders motivate, listen, and so on, they've been extremely receptive because they realize that to compete in the world market with multinationals that are already using these styles of leadership, they are going to have to make the shift themselves. So China, to my surprise, is actually quite receptive.

Interestingly, Chinese business has always valued relationships and networks. Companies in the United States and the United Kingdom have spent recent decades trying to squeeze all emotion out of the workplace.

That was a rather foolish endeavor because we don't ever leave our emotions at home when we go to work. They were always there; they were just squelched or ignored, sometimes at a disastrous cost. Most Asian cultures are quite relationship-oriented, and business has always been based on relationships as you say, which means many of these skills are natural in the culture. On the other hand, India, perhaps because it was a British colony, had very strong command and control structures among the business class. But most businesses, even large corporations, are family-owned businesses even today. And the culture was similar to that in China but for different historical reasons. So they both need to make the shift. On the other hand, the way you do business—as opposed to the structure of the company but how people and especially entrepreneurs do business—is very relationship-oriented, so a number of these skills come quite naturally.

Does emotional intelligence in leaders provide any protection against the sorts of excesses we have seen in the corporate world: Enron and many others?

One of the fundamental capabilities that distinguish emotionally intelligent leaders from others is integrity. Business needs to make a pendulum swing from a culture where whatever is legal and whatever accounting would approve was done—that is, a culture where it is very hard to raise ethical concerns—to one where ethics becomes a business advantage. That requires leaders who are ethical, and that has always been a part of the emotional intelligence model.

How does it go down in a tractor plant in Nebraska where people aren't used to hearing about the more touchy-feely stuff?

It's not touchy-feely; that's a misconception. This is being intelligent about emotions, not being emotional. I'm not saying that people should necessarily express emotions openly and fluently. I'm saying that you should be able to manage your distressing emotions so that they don't get in the way of the work you have to do. And you need to do that because there is a relationship between the emotional centers of the brain which pump out your distressing emotions and the neocortex, prefrontal brain, which needs to take in information and understand it clearly and respond flexibly. The more you are under the sway of the emotional centers, the less nimble and the more paralyzed your thinking brain becomes. So it's because of that reciprocal relationship that you need to be able to manage emotions. And you need to be able to manage relationships effectively, too. That goes down just fine in Nebraska. If you say let's be touchy-feely, then you are not talking about what I'm talking about. I wouldn't even mention it in Nebraska.

Where can your ideas make the biggest impact? Is it at the sales interface or in the boardroom?

At every level where leadership is operating. So it could be at the team level, among the team members—in fact there is team emotional intelligence. A woman named Vanessa Druskat [assistant professor of organizational behavior at the Weatherhead School of Management] has shown that these same abilities operate at the collective level in a team and distinguish high-performance teams from low-performance teams. It's distributed. So anywhere that people need to work together to achieve a collective goal, it is required.

The Sales Guy

Author, journalist, speechwriter, political aide, capturer of the business zeitgeist; Daniel Pink is or has been all these and more. Along the way, Pink has written four books. In *Free Agent Nation: The Future of Working for Yourself*, he was one of the first to celebrate the generation of self-employed workers. Freed from conventional corporate life, he argued, a growing number of people were liberated by the Internet to lead fulfilling and productive lives on their own terms. In *The Adventures of Johnny Bunko: The Last Career Guide You'll Ever Need*, Pink welded the Japanese manga cartoons to the business book genre to produce another bestseller. *A Whole New Mind: Why Right-Brainers Will Rule the Future* looks at the power of creative thinking in the modern business world. *Drive: The Surprising Truth About What Motivates Us* argues that we need to abandon the ineffectual carrot and stick approach and stresses the importance of doing something we love for a career.

This was followed by *To Sell Is Human: The Surprising Truth About Moving Others*. In this book Pink examines one of the most neglected corners of managerial life: selling.

We all live by selling something, Robert Louis Stevenson said, and of course it's true, but in reality a lot of people have a perception of sales as being slightly tawdry, slightly seedy. Why do you think that is?

Well, I would argue that it's more than slightly tawdry and seedy. People really have a visceral distaste for it, and I think that tells us a lot more about the conditions in which sales have long taken place than about sales itself. Most of what we know about sales from Robert Louis Stevenson's time to just a few years ago comes from a world of information asymmetry where the seller always had a lot more information than the buyer. When the seller has a lot more information than the buyer, the seller can rip you off.

One of the most important papers in economics over the last 50 years is by Dan and George Akerlof, "The Market for Lemons," which was about information asymmetry in used car markets. For a long time the seller always had an enormous information advantage over the buyer. What's more, the buyer didn't have any choices. The buyer had no way to talk back; therefore, sellers can take the low road. They can be sleazy, slimy, and manipulative.

This is the whole reason we have the principle of buyer beware. This principle comes from information asymmetry. In the last few years that world of information asymmetry has started to end.

Now buyers can know as much as sellers. In some ways, in automobiles, you can go into a new car lot and you can arguably know more than the seller of the car. You can arguably know more about a Ford Focus than that Ford Focus dealer. You can go to a Ford Focus users group and find out all the idiosyncrasies. You can find out what other dealers in the area are charging. And so we've gone from a world where buyers have not many choices, very little information, and no way to talk back to a world where buyers have lots of choices, as much information as the sellers, and all kinds of ways to talk back. That's a very different world. That to me is a world of seller beware.

Seller beware is a different enterprise altogether. The interesting thing is that we actually spend more time selling than we realize. In the United States about 1 in 9 people work in sales; in the United Kingdom it is 1 in 10; in Australia it's about 1 in 9. In most similarly situated countries it's somewhere between 1 in 9 and 1 in 10. But I just did some research showing that the other 8 in 9 or the 9 in 10 spend huge portions of their time in what I like to call nonsales selling. They're persuading, influencing, convincing, cajoling. They're saying, Let's make an exchange. You give something up, I give something up, and we're both going to be better off. It's sales with a twist. It's sales except that money's not changing hands and the transaction isn't denominated in dollars, pounds, or euros; it's denominated in attention or effort or time or commitment or energy. It's things like pitching your idea at a meeting. It's things like bosses trying to get their employees to do different things or do things in different ways. It's one person in a firm trying to rally other people to join her team rather than someone else's team, and we have data showing that people are spending about 40 percent of their time on the job doing this.

So like it or not, we're all in sales, but sales isn't what it used to be. We're in a world of information parity, which is a world of seller beware, and that requires fundamentally different skills.

There are a number of different things that have changed. First, the rise of small entrepreneurs everywhere has put more people into a sales role. Entrepreneurs sell. Period. That's what they do. They're selling to funders. They're selling to employees: come and work for us. They're selling to customers, obviously. And so the rise of small entrepreneurs has put more people in selling.

The other thing is what's going on inside traditional established firms. It used to be that functions were very much segmented. You did marketing, I did operations, she did sales, he did human resources, and everybody swam in his or her own lane. That works very well for very stable, predictable business conditions, which we no longer have, and so now you have much greater elasticity across borders.

An American company called Palantir Technologies is a $300 million a year company. It has a billion dollar evaluation. So it does $300 million a year in sales and has no salespeople. In other companies like this, generally smaller start-up companies that have literally hundreds and millions of dollars in sales with no salespeople, when you ask them why they don't have salespeople, they give you this Zen-like answer of no one's in sales because everyone's in sales. They don't see it as a discrete function. They see it as more elastic, and so everybody does, but then no one does. It's a strange world.

What's interesting is that businesses carve out other things as discrete functions but haven't carved out sales as a discrete function because they consider it part of everybody's job.

The job increases over the last 10 years have been in education and healthcare, which are all about moving other people. It's all about persuading, influencing, convincing people in a nonsales way. It's unavoidable. Even people who had a distaste for sales, didn't really want to think about it, tried to push it aside, now have to reckon with the fact that like it or not, they're in sales. The good news is that you don't have to be a sleazy, slimy, smarmy, deceitful, manipulative cad in order to do it well.

What are the requirements of this brave new world?
There's a rich trove of social science, although much of it doesn't deal with sales directly. But if you go deep and wide enough into this body of research, you can begin to get some clues. What I found are three foundational qualities, the new ABCs: A, attunement; B, buoyancy; and C, clarity.

Attunement is perspective taken. Can I take your point of view rather than my point of view? Can I get out of the anchor of my own position and see the world from someone else's point of view?

Then there's B, buoyancy. One of the salesmen I interviewed has this lovely, very poetic phrase. He said the hardest part about being in sales is that every day you face an ocean of rejection. That is a lot. It's not a puddle of rejection or a pond of rejection, it's an ocean of rejection, and buoyancy is how you stay afloat in that ocean of rejection. And the science gives us some clues about what to do before an encounter, what to do during an encounter, and what to do after an encounter.

Finally there's C, clarity. Having access to information doesn't give anybody a comparative advantage. What matters more is being able to distill information, share information, separate out the signal and the noise in information, but also, very important, move from purely solving existing problems to identifying new problems, going from problem solving to problem finding, which is a very different and much more artistic skill. So those are the foundational qualities: attunement, buoyancy, and clarity.

On top of those foundational qualities are the particular tactical skills, which are to pitch, to improvise, and to serve. We're pitching all the time. I'm pitching right now. We're pitching all the time. When we send an e-mail, we're pitching. When we send a tweet, we're pitching. And we've always talked about what in America is called the elevator pitch.

There are some other interesting ways in which science tells us how to pitch. For instance, questions have a particular power when we pitch. It should be used sparingly, but there's some really remarkable evidence showing that rhymes are extremely effective in pitching. There's some interesting research from Carnegie Mellon about what makes an effective e-mail subject line, because every e-mail is a pitch.

You talk about Twitter as a pitch.
Actually, once again, asking questions through Twitter is a very effective thing to do. Some of us might roll our eyes a bit at self-promotion, but a lot of Twitter readers don't mind self-promotion if it's providing useful information. So retweeting someone saying that I'm awesome isn't that useful, but retweeting someone saying I'm going to be signing books at such and such a place on Thursday is actually fairly useful.

Improvisation is another interesting one, because a lot of sales training focuses on overcoming objections. That's a key point there. How do you overcome objections? Most of the training ends up being very scripted. I memorize my pitch, I memorize the 27 most likely objections, and then I memorize the 54 ways to overcome those objections. And that scripted approach is just really not effective but is very much an industrial legacy.

Now I think you're better off improvising. This is what you have to do when your perfectly attuned, appropriately buoyant, superclear picture goes awry, as it will in the first three minutes. And lessons of improvisational theater will give us some really important clues.

What I found really powerful for myself is hearing offers. Improv artists are taught to hear offers, so when two actors are on stage in an improv setting, anything you say is an offer. That's really, really effective in communication in general. The principle, really important too in improv, is to make your partner look good. If you and I are on a stage together, my job is to make you look good. Your job is to make me look good. That works out reasonably well.

And then finally, serve. Forty years ago Robert Greenleaf came up with this concept of servant leadership, which has been, I don't want to say embraced, but has filtered its way into the consciousness, and I think many good people subscribe to that idea that leaders serve first and lead second. And now I think we're in a world of servant selling where the most effective thing to do, not only the most noble, the most moral, but the most effective thing to do, is to serve first and sell later. It's a very different approach to selling in the way that Greenleaf came up with, a very different approach to leadership.

CHAPTER 10

Managing
Millennials

We have seen that there is a huge challenge facing managers in engaging with employees. Research by the economist Richard Layard found that people were less happy interacting with their bosses than with any others in their lives. Loneliness was deemed a better option than communicating with the supposed leader.

The issues that this raises are broader than management. Politicians and many others in societies worldwide are trying to figure out the best means of utilizing the often latent power of people. Nowhere is this truer than in the management of the emerging generations entering the workplace. Generation Y, the millennial generation born after 1980, offers unique managerial and organizational challenges.

Offering their insights into what managers can and can't do in managing millennials are Tammy Erickson and Lynda Gratton. Putting it into action is Vineet Nayar, CEO of the Indian company HCL.

Erickson is an author and expert on organizations and the changing workforce and, in particular, the generational differences between workers. She has also done extensive research on how corporations innovate through collaboration.

Who are Generation Y, and what makes this generation different?

My recent work looks at how people born between about 1985 and 2000, Generation Y, are different from older workers. Because they grew up at a time when events such as terrorism and school violence were very much in the news, they tend to think in terms of how to make the most out of today and make sure that what they are doing is meaningful, interesting, and challenging. They are a little less likely to defer gratification than are some of the other generations.

What are some of the defining characteristics of Generation Y?

One of the things that I talk about is immediacy being a defining characteristic for this generation; I think it's very easy to mistake that for pure impatience. We say they're impatient; they want everything now. But I believe they're just living in the moment, and, in a sense, they're responding to the world we gave them. It was a world in which they would be likely to come to the conclusion that they better make the most of what they have right now.

How many Generation Y workers are there?

It's a big generation. We're talking about a lot of people: a quarter of the world's population. The percentages differ a bit as you go around the world. In Europe the proportion of Gen Y to the total population is a little lower; obviously, in Asia, it's a huge percentage of the population. Make no mistake: they are going to be a great force in a company because they bring a lot of good skills.

Are they formally educated, all college graduates?

Only about a quarter of them are finishing college. Our economies are changing faster than our educational systems. The jobs that are being created are very heavily weighted toward people who have a college education, but we haven't switched our educational patterns to keep pace with that. So we actually have an alarming situation developing in which we'll have a shortage of people with higher-level skills and, unfortunately, a surplus of undereducated people.

So three out of four have never been to college?

I should qualify that statement by saying that a lot of these people start college, but they're not necessarily following it through to the end. Interestingly, it's skewed; girls tend to finish more than boys, and some of that, I think, is a sense of relevance. A lot of the boys I interviewed felt they had opportunities available to them but that the college classes just weren't relevant to achieving what they wanted to achieve.

What would you say is the major difference between Generation Y people and the rest of the workforce?
A major difference in this generation is that they could well have a life expectancy of up to 120 years, so they're going to be around for a while. That contributes a bit to something I think older people get annoyed with: this generation tends to be looking at their twenties as a time of experimentation. So when we say buckle down, get a good job, they're responding, I have a lot of time. That's a much more relaxed attitude than past generations had.

How does that translate to a challenge for managers?
The differences in attitude and experiences of this group mean that organizations will have to lead them differently. A couple of things come to mind. First, don't overspecify things; they love to figure things out for themselves. These are people who have gone through school not necessarily reading a textbook from start to finish but getting a snippet of information from here and there. So I don't recommend overtraining them: give them a challenge and let them figure it out.

Are there other key differences?

Second, a very interesting difference I found involves their attitude toward feedback. I don't know what feedback means to you, but if somebody says that he or she is going to give me feedback, that sends a bit of a cold chill down my spine, because it usually means I'm going to be judged in some way, assessed. Generation Y doesn't see that at all: feedback has a totally different meaning. For them, feedback is a tip, it's coaching, and it's something they want all the time, multiple times a day. So you can now witness some funny organizational situations in which a senior person will say, "Look, kid, I told you; you're doing fine!" But it's not enough for Generation Y; the young person wants more and more bits of feedback.

What is the best way to communicate with them?

This generation communicates differently. We need to understand that fact in order to communicate with them. One of their most striking characteristics is that they coordinate whereas we schedule. If you were going to get together with a friend for dinner, you'd probably call in advance; you'd probably decide on a time and a place you were going to meet. They wouldn't do any of that. They'd wait until the moment and then would send a message, probably by text instead of trying to connect voice to voice. But the interesting thing is that even then, the message would not say, "Let's meet"; it would say, "Where are you?" It would be a request for your coordinates.

Then they would text back their coordinates and begin a process of homing in on each other, like ships with radar, until they met up at a particular place. They're coordinators. Also, they love to text message. Often they prefer to text rather than talk.

In a group that has multiple generations, how should a manager begin to meld them into a team?
A leader with Generation Y employees needs to make some things explicit that older workers take for granted. I recommend that the manager have a conversation with the entire group. Assuming that most groups are going to be mixed, the manager should put assumptions on the table. For example, he or she should discuss how the team is going to communicate with one another, what will be considered as "office hours," what the start time for the day is (and be precise: does everyone have to come in at eight or eight-thirty?). Those are workplace issues this generation doesn't understand much about, so bring those kinds of normative behaviors out into the open: encourage the team to have a conversation if the manager's rules are difficult for some to understand or accept. Decide which rules are something you must have, and yes, they'll adapt; they'll live by them. But I think you have to make them clear.

Do Generation Y workers truly fit into a team?
This brings up another area in which I've done a lot of research beyond Generation Y: the subject of col-

laborative teamwork. I have worked a great deal with Lynda Gratton of London Business School. We did one large study that looked at intact team collaboration to try to determine what correlated with teams that successfully work together. We found out that diversity works against collaboration. If you and I are different in just about any way—generationally, politically, educationally—that will make collaboration more difficult, if not impossible.

Impossible?

Perhaps. The kinds of things that help with collaboration include forming trust-based relationships so that workers have to get to know each other in some way. Companies can facilitate that by providing networking opportunities. But interestingly, there were some very, I would say, hard-edged things as well: you have to have efficient processes. Collaboration is a discretionary activity. A worker can think, "I don't have to do it if I don't want to; you can't make me." And so to encourage such a worker, a company needs to make it easy to collaborate. If it's really difficult, I'm just going to take off and work somewhere else. It also helps build collaboration if all team members have a clearly defined role.

What about the fact that many team members today work in different geographic locations?

If they're working at a distance from one another, a leader needs to provide a basis for them to get to know one another. Technology helps, but at least for many older workers today, it's not enough. I would suggest that managers need a physical meeting to get that to happen. They need to make sure roles are clear, they need to make sure that the process of collaborating is easy, and they need to role-model what it means to be a team player. That makes a big difference.

Do you find that the concept of retirement is changing with each new generation?

I think retirement is an outdated notion. One of my previous books was on this subject. We're seeing more and more that individuals, even if they officially retire from the system, are keeping busy in different ways. A lot of that book was about helping boomers think about the kinds of lives they'd like to lead after official retirement. What Generation Y might think about retirement is still a work in progress.

This sounds like quite a revolutionary change in the concept of being a worker.

In many ways, today's workers are changing the workplace. One of the problems organizations have is that they are based on a twentieth-century model, sometimes even a nineteenth-century model. For example, people are racing to put in place collaborative technology, but they're going to run right up against these nineteenth-century organizations. Collaboration, in fact, goes against about five centuries of management practice and theory, and it certainly affects our younger generations in terms of their ability to feel comfortable and fit in, so that is the kind of thing we need to think about. Organizations in the past were based on an equation that essentially traded loyalty to the organization and the boss for protection and care. That's not a collaborative concept but leads to silo kinds of behavior, and so organizations need to begin to break that equation with different kinds of arrangements with employees.

Can you provide an example of that?

Surely. Many traditional organizations have a culture in which management basically endorses this viewpoint among workers: "You do your job, I'll do mine, and by the way, mind your own business." So it would be impolite in many companies for me to comment directly to you on the quality of your work. I might gossip a bit, but I wouldn't talk to you directly about it. That won't work in a collaborative organization. So there are lots of behavioral things that we need to address head on in order to begin to shift organizations both to take advantage of collaborative technology and to welcome younger members of the workforce.

You mentioned earlier that you are optimistic about the generations now shaping the workplace. Still feel that way?

I do feel optimistic, perhaps for a reason we haven't touched on yet, which is the missing generation: Gen

X [people born during the late 1960s and the 1970s]. My third book—it's actually the last of a trilogy—will be about Gen X. I started that research, I have to admit, a little skeptical. My initial interviews with Gen Xers were a bit shocking to me as a boomer. But over the course of several years of research, I really came to appreciate and respect Gen Xs. Their values are very different from mine, the way they approach things. For example, one man told me that boomers are intent on climbing the beanstalk: "You just want to get as high as you can go." He continued, "I'm worried about the base of the beanstalk. I want to make sure that it's as sturdy and as broad as it can be." I think that's a pretty good characterization of the difference. Gen X workers think in terms of options, what-ifs. What would I do if this were to happen? Have I got a backup plan? They're very thoughtful about keeping multiple balls in the air at the same time, whereas boomers may be much more full steam ahead toward one goal. Given our world today, given the challenges we face, I think Gen Xs are going to be fantastic leaders. I think they actually bring the mindset that we need to lead our organizations in new directions over the next several decades. That makes me feel optimistic.

All Together Now

Central to the challenge and appeal of the new generation entering the workforce is their very different approach to work and very different attitudes toward it. This is having major repercussions on how organizations actually go about the daily grind of managing their activities.

Lynda Gratton from London Business School has charted these changes over recent years as part of her work with the Future Work Forum and her Hot Spots Movement. Core to what she is witnessing, she explains, is a shift from competition to collaboration.

There seems to be a thread that connects your work about the move from business as a competitive arena to a far more collaborative place.

Yes, I think it's actually one of the most important moves that we have seen over the last couple of decades, and I think it's accelerating. The truth is that competition is always about fighting about a piece of cake, whereas the really, really important thing to do is to make the cake bigger, and to do that you need to cooperate. So I believe cooperation is really one of the most important issues facing organizations right now.

These pockets of collaboration or pockets of cooperation are things you call hot spots?

Yes; when we looked at a lot at organizations, what we found was that quite often you just see business as usual—you can almost imagine that as being green—and then sometimes the place really freezes up—you can almost imagine it as blue icicles. Then, as you watch, you see these incredible places of energy and innovation—you can imagine them as orange or red—and we call those hot spots.

How do you know when you're in a hot spot?
Think about a time when you felt really energized and innovated at work. How did you feel? The first thing is that the level of conversation really goes up and people immediately talk about feeling energized, feeling excited, feeling as if they trusted the people around them, feeling as if there was something there that really helped them focus. Also, they talk about diversity, which is very interesting; they almost always say: when I'm in a hot spot, the people around me are different from me.

Some companies are better at creating hot spots than others. What are the factors that you've found in your research that make a difference?
We have masses of research on this; we now have pretty much the largest database in the world on communities and teams in terms of their energy. What we found was that there's not a simple answer. Actually, energy and innovation are created at three levels. They're created at the level of the individual: Am I prepared to cooperate? Am I prepared to build networks? Do I have a vision?

They're created at the level of the team. The team is really important in terms of the way it works together, the way it manages conflict, but the context is also important. By context, I mean, Do people see senior executives role-modeling, being innovative and energized? Are the pay processes supporting that? Are they trained to do that? So organizations have to think about those three levels.

Give us an example of an organization that does this well.
It's really difficult generally to make any judgments about what organizations are great at because context changes, leadership changes.

The other difference is that if you're not careful, you only talk about young companies, you talk about Google, you talk about eBay, when in fact most people work in large, old companies. If you want to look at great innovative practices, look at Tata Consultancy Services in Mumbai, or look at what Infosys is doing, or look at what some of the Chinese companies are doing.

I think what's really exciting about best practice is that it's spreading. It's now a global phenomenon; it's not just a Western phenomenon.

Do you find that some of these Eastern companies, with slightly different philosophical roots, do it differently, or is it the same, or does every company do it slightly differently?
We've now done a whole year of research looking at global trends, and actually, multinationals are more like themselves than they are like the country they are in. So there isn't an Indian way of doing it. What I would say is that if you look at Tata Consultancy Services or you

look at Infosys or Wipro, it's an IT knowledge-based way of doing it. So they do things in a rather similar way to how you would see Apple doing things.

So what I'm suggesting is that in terms of practice, that's also becoming a global phenomenon. There is an argument that Chinese companies, because of the Confucian way of thinking, are more cooperative. We actually haven't seen evidence of that. The data that we collected in Singapore in particular showed that levels of cooperation in Asian teams aren't any higher than in Western teams. What really makes a difference is the company, not the country.

Your book after Hot Spots, *titled* Glow, *was very much taking that to the individual level, so you were beginning to talk about how we can empower ourselves to have our own little hot spots.*

One of the reasons I wrote *Glow* is that like many other people who are professors of business, I've really only ever talked about organizations in the books I've written. This was my first attempt at writing a book for people. My background is as a psychologist, so I've always been interested in thinking about organizations from the inside out, from individuals, and building up.

So what I tried to do in *Glow* was to really think about what it would take for an individual to be energized, to be in a hot spot, given what we know about hot spots. So basically, the themes that I talked about were "How do you learn to be cooperative?"

because I think that that's something you can learn to do. How do you build valuable networks that help you to link into diverse groups? And how do you find something within yourself that's going to energize and excite both yourself and other people?

How do you lead in a collaborative environment?

Being a cooperative leader, and we have very clear research about this, means not so much what you say but what you do; it's about how you personally are perceived to be in terms of cooperation; it's about understanding that the way you manage others is through inspiration; and it's about realizing that your networks and the networks that you encourage others to build are also going to be really crucial.

How do you communicate a collaborative mindset?

One of the companies that we looked at was Standard Chartered Bank, and they said cooperation is really important. And I said, Well, how do you role model that as a leader? They said: One of the interesting things is that if you go around any of our offices around the world, almost always you'll see a picture of the bank's top team standing together. Words are really important, but the big communication thing is how people see you behave, the stories that you're prepared to tell, and the language that you use. One of the things I've done is to look at the language leaders use. The language of cooperation is a language of *we*. You use the word *colleagues*, you use the word *peer*, you use the word *together*. The language of competition is *I*, and then the stories you tell are about battlefields and winner and losers and blood and dying. Leaders show who they are as soon as they open their mouths.

Let's talk about the future of work.

We identified the five areas that we think are going to be really important for the future: demographic shifts, carbon and resources, globalization, technology, and societal changes. For each one of those we did an in-depth data collection to ask, What do we know is happening? Then we got 200 executives from around the world and used some sophisticated community-building technology learned from our friends at Nokia to get this group to start talking about the future, about the hard facts we'd shown them.

Then we brought them together—in Singapore, in London, in various other places—and said, What does this mean to you? And they'd begun to build vignettes, little ideas of what would it be like in 2020, 2030, 2040. We made those into videos, and then we began to see what they loved about the future and what made them really fearful. That, for me, has been so energizing, to see that people are worried about the future but they're also optimistic, and to help them think about what their future is going to be. What do you say to your children? And if you're a leader, what do you say to your employees and what do you say to your successors?

Have you extended that to talking to young people coming into the workplace, because obviously we've got this web generation, whatever you want to call them, but they're going to be very different, they're going to have different expectations?

Absolutely. And to that point, each of the 22 companies that participated in our research nominated 10 people. We asked all to nominate at least two people in their mid-twenties.

My view is that Gen Y will change work. One thing we know about them is that they take a much more clear view about the lives they want and the companies they want to work with and the work they want to do. I suspect that they will be a huge driver for change.

There's no question there are some really difficult challenges ahead, but I believe in the empathy and good-naturedness, potentially, of Gen Y; the fact that 5 billion people are going to be linked up by 2020; and the sorts of conversations that are going on globally at the moment, which will create a very positive future.

Employees First

Vineet Nayar is the vice chairman and joint managing director of the Indian company HCL Technologies Ltd., a $4.4 billion global information and technology company. He is also the author of *Employees First, Customers Second*; that is why he first caught our eye at the Thinkers50. We are always interested in practitioners who have taken the time to reflect on and capture their management philosophy and techniques in books or articles. These are the visionary practitioners.

With Nayar at the helm, HCL has cut a defiant swath through management orthodoxy by proclaiming that employees rather than customers should come first. His work offers a compelling new take on management and in particular on how organizations should manage and motivate millennials.

There is a perennial search in the world of business research. We want the human side of the hard stuff, the stories behind the dry financial analysis, and hard stats to accompany the soft people side of business.

They don't come any softer than HCL Technologies. Its philosophy is distilled down to two words: *Employees First*, "a unique management approach that unshackles the creative energies of our 85,335 plus employees and puts this collective force to work in the service of customers' business problems."

In practice, this means that there is an emphasis on transparency. HCL rates managers on aspects of their performance: strategic vision, ability to communicate, problem-solving skills, responsiveness, and so on. There is nothing unusual in running such a process. What is unusual is that the results of the survey—the numbers and the comments—are aggregated and published online for every employee to look at.

It may be soft, but HCL is highly successful. Hard performance figures validate its softly, softly approach. Indeed, HCL has numbers aplenty to back up its humanity. Its 2012 results saw revenue reach $4.1 billion, up more than 17 percent; there was a fivefold increase in $100 million–plus clients; and during that year, Eli Lilly, a global pharmaceutical corporation, and HCL opened a Co-Innovation Lab in Singapore for developing novel technologies.

Among more than 3,000 technology companies in the Bloomberg database, there are only 7 with revenue of more than $2.5 billion, a market capitalization of more than $5 billion, and a compound annual growth rate greater than 25 percent during the last five years. HCL Technologies is one of those seven.

The Art of Rafting

Stopping off at HCL's London office—one of HCL's 31 world-wide—to explain the hard facts and hard work that lie behind the soft stuff, Vineet Nayar is bearishly affable. "Six hundred percent growth in seven years; what else can you ask for?" he observes with a smile. "Employees first gave us a competitive advantage."

Vineet Nayar joined HCL in 1985 as a management trainee and worked his way up through the company, becoming president of HCL Technologies (there is also a sister company, HCL Infosystems) in 2005.

We suggest that growth brings its own problems. Another Indian giant, Infosys, is currently struggling to come to terms with its decelerating growth rate even though in these straitened times its growth remains comparatively healthy. Headlong growth brings expectations, at the very least. Nayar has little truck with the concept of growth providing problems. "Challenges," he corrects. "If you start seeing challenges as challenges and not as opportunities, then you should not be in management. If you're an F1 racing car driver, then do you see bends as opportunities or do you see bends as threats?

"The history of HCL is a bet on the growth of technology services. Back in the late 1990s, 45 percent of our revenues came from technology development. We were very good at what we did. But when the technology meltdown happened in 2000, technology spending vanished overnight. So we had to reinvent our business model. We took a look at our market space, and the key trend was that there was too much emphasis on volume and people had forgotten the concept of value. Everybody was rushing to India, but no one was asking, 'Am I getting value?' I believed that down the line clients would get frustrated: 'I have got my 30 percent, 40 percent cost saving; now what?'"

HCL decided to position itself as a value-centric company rather than a volume-centric company. "We decided to chase deals where we were both important to the customer and creating value for them," Nayar explains.

Nayar believes that the global slowdown from 2008 has played right into HCL's responsive hands. "So you are the team which rows in still waters better than anybody else. That's fine. Now suddenly there's turbulence, and you need to do river rafting. Most companies keep crying that the environment is not good for rowing—our rowing skills are not being used, and we're waiting for the environment to settle down so we can row again. No. Managers cannot be married to what they are good at. They have to be good at what the environment seeks from them. Otherwise they should step out of the way and let somebody else do what is required. The time is to river raft, to start intuitively driving the boat, and there is an opportunity. At HCL we need to become the best river rafter in town."

As a closing metaphor, whitewater rafting may be the best summation of what contemporary management demands of all those involved in it: adaptability, huge amounts of strength and skill, and an element of good fortune.

Notes

Chapter 1

1. Drucker, Peter, "Management's New Paradigms," *Forbes*, October 5, 1998.
2. Farnham, Alan, "The Man Who Changed Work Forever," *Fortune*, July 21, 1997.
3. Pascale, Richard, *Managing on the Edge*, Penguin, London, 1990.
4. Follett, Mary Parker, *Dynamic Administration* (ed. Elliot M. Fox and Urwick Lyndall), Harper, 1941.

Chapter 2

1. Khurana, Rakesh, and Nohria, Nitin, "It's Time to Make Management a True Profession," *Harvard Business Review*, October 2008.

Chapter 4

1. Ford, Henry, *My Life and Work*, William Heinemann, London, 1923.
2. Deming, W. Edwards, speech, Tokyo, Japan, November 1985.

Chapter 6

1. Schein, Edgar H., "Leadership and Organizational Culture," in Frances Hesselbein, Marshall Goldsmith, and Richard Beckhard (eds.), *The Leader of the Future*, Jossey-Bass, 1996.
2. Ibid.
3. Ibid.
4. Kotter, John, "Leading Change: Why Transformation Efforts Fail," *Harvard Business Review*, 1995.
5. Kanter, Rosabeth Moss, "The Enduring Skills of Change Leaders," *Leader to Leader*, Summer, 1999.
6. Ibid.
7. Kanter, Rosabeth Moss, "Leadership and the Psychology of Turnarounds," *Harvard Business Review*, June 2003.

Chapter 7

1. Michaels, Ed, Handfield-Jones, Helen, and Axelroad, Beth, *The War for Talent*, Harvard Business Press, 2001.
2. Ibid.
3. Goffee, Rob, and Jones, Gareth, "Leading Clever People," *Harvard Business Review*, March 2007; *Clever*, Harvard Business Press, 2009.

Acknowledgments

We would like to thank Steve Coomber for his help with this book. At Thinkers50 we are grateful to our colleagues Joan Bigham and Deb Harrity for their essential and creative contributions. We would also like to thank all the people we have interviewed over the last 20 years writing about business thinking, in particular, Jim Champy, Tammy Erickson, Howard Gardner, Daniel Goleman, Lynda Gratton, Gary Hamel, Sylvia Ann Hewlett, Rosabeth Moss Kanter, John Kotter, Rakesh Khurana, Erin Meyer, Vineet Nayar, David Norton, Henry Mintzberg, Dan Pink, Doug Ready, Steve Spear, and Fons Trompenaars.

Index

About the Authors

Adjunct professors at IE Business School in Madrid, Stuart Crainer and Des Dearlove create and champion business ideas. They are the creators of Thinkers50 (www.thinkers50 .com), the original global ranking of business thought leaders. Their work in this area led *Management Today* to describe them as "market makers par excellence."

As journalists and commentators, Stuart and Des have been asking difficult questions for more than two decades. Now, they help leaders come up with their own wicked questions and explore how best to engage with people and communicate the answers. They were advisors to the 2009 British government report on employee engagement, and associates of the Management Innovation Lab at London Business School.

Their clients include Swarovski, the Department of Economic Development in Abu Dhabi, Fujitsu, and Heidrick & Struggles.

Stuart and Des have been columnists at the *Times* (London), contributing editors to the American magazine *Strategy+Business*, and edited the bestselling *Financial Times Handbook of Management*. Their books include *The Management Century*, *Gravy Training*, *The Future of Leadership*, and *Generation Entrepreneur*. These books are available in more than 20 languages.

Stuart is editor of *Business Strategy Review*. According to *Personnel Today*, he is one of the most influential figures in British people management. Des is an associate fellow of Saïd Business School at Oxford University and is the author of a bestselling study on the leadership style of Richard Branson.

Des and Stuart have taught MBA students, professors, and senior executives in programs all over the world. These include the Oxford Strategic Leadership Programme at the Saïd Business School at Oxford University; Columbia Business School in New York; the Tuck Business School at Dartmouth College in New Hampshire; IMD in Lausanne, Switzerland; and London Business School.

About the Thinkers50

The Thinkers50, the definitive global ranking of management thinkers, scans, ranks, and shares management ideas. It was the brainchild of Stuart Crainer and Des Dearlove, two business journalists, who identified a place in the market for an independent ranking of the top management thinkers. First published in 2001, the Thinkers50 has been published every two years since.

In 2011, Crainer and Dearlove added a number of award categories and hosted the first ever Thinkers50 Summit, described as "the Oscars of Management Thinking." The 2011 winner was Harvard Business School's Professor Clayton Christensen. The previous winners were C. K. Prahalad (2009 and 2007), Michael Porter (2005), and Peter Drucker (2003 and 2001).

The ranking is based on voting at the Thinkers50 website and input from a team of advisors led by Stuart Crainer and Des Dearlove. The Thinkers50 has 10 established criteria by which thinkers are evaluated:

- Originality of ideas
- Practicality of ideas
- Presentation style
- Written communication
- Loyalty of followers
- Business sense
- International outlook
- Rigor of research
- Impact of ideas
- Power to inspire